Fordham University & the United States:
A History
By Debra Caruso Marrone

e·LITBOOKS

New York

Caruso Marrone, Debra, 1959-
Fordham University & the United States: A History
Includes bibliographical references and index.
ISBN   978-0-9894011-1-1 (pbck)
          978-0-9894011-2-8 (E-Book)
1. History. 2. Education.   2013

*Dedicated to my mother, Isabel Lettieri Caruso,
whose love of books was immeasurable.*

Table of Contents

Introduction

Most of those associated with Fordham University, originally St. John's College, know the basic history of its founding, the glory athletic days with Vince Lombardi and the Seven Blocks of Granite, its involvement in World War II and what went on during the turbulent 60's. This book will discuss a bit of that (just a bit) and a lot more.

Fordham, its graduates and faculty have played a significant role in U.S. history. That was the intent of Archbishop John Hughes who was resolute in his belief that there should be a major Catholic college in New York City. He was ordered by the Pope to make that happen. In a very short time, Hughes fulfilled his vision to create an institution of great stature and influence.

Photo: Fordham Archives

Archbishop John Hughes

We will examine highlights of the university's past and discuss Fordham in the context of the nation, as it became a dominant force around the globe. When you're finished reading, you'll have a more robust view of the university's storied history and an appreciation of its place in the world.

Did you know that Senator Robert F. Kennedy was scheduled to be the Fordham commencement speaker in June of 1968, but he was tragically assassinated in Los Angeles three days before his planned speech?

In fact, three U.S. presidents received honorary degrees from Fordham – Franklin Delano Roosevelt (1929), Harry S. Truman

(1946) and John F. Kennedy (1958). Two visited the campus as president.

Or, are you aware that a former Fordham student, Colonel Robert Gould Shaw, led one of the first Black regiments during the Civil War? Matthew Broderick starred in a big Hollywood movie about him that featured the university's most famous graduate, Denzel Washington.

Consider that the university campus grew to 300 acres, but in 1885, the university was ordered to sell 215 acres to New York City so it could build the New York Botanical Gardens and the Bronx Zoo. For almost 60 years prior, Fordham students had direct access to the Bronx River for swimming and fishing.

Nearly 175 years since its inception, whether you're an alumnus or you've been a visitor to the campus, the story of Fordham's past will come to life and you will echo the thoughts of Thomas Gaffney Taaffe in his 1891 book, *A History of St. John's College,* written for the 50th anniversary jubilee:

"Fordham College of today is indeed a beautiful place, but one who, in addition to its natural beauties, finds every foot of ground, every rock and tree, every nook and corner of its time-stained walls reminiscent of some little incident of the happy days of long ago, it becomes a veritable Arcadia. What old student, returning, can gaze on the familiar scenes without a pang of regret for the days that are no more, and the pleasures and companions that, alike, are but memories of a dim, uncertain past.

"But apart from the charm it possesses in the eyes of its loving children, Fordham stands pre-eminent among institutions of its kind for the picturesqueness of its surroundings, unrivaled in the beauty of its grounds. Less than a dozen miles from the heart of the great metropolis, it might be leagues away from the busy hum of men, such is the peace and quietude that pervade the spot."

Some would argue that Fordham today is enjoying its heyday, as there were many trials and tribulations involved in operating the school from its beginnings through the better part of two centuries. Under Father Joseph McShane, Fordham is bigger, richer and as prestigious as it's ever been.

I hope you'll be interested to know that proceeds from the sale of this book go to the Fordham College Alumni Association, which provides scholarships and grants to Fordham College students. So, please recommend this book to others.

Chapter I:
A Vision Becomes Reality

In 1839 Rev. John J. Hughes, CoAdjutor Bishop (later Archbishop) of the Roman Catholic Diocese of New York, bought 98 acres, called Rose Hill Manor, in what was then Westchester for $29,750. He spent an additional $10,000 to convert the home and farm into a seminary and school named St. John's College.

The larger land, 3,900 acres, was originally the domain of the Mohegan Indians, and is believed to have been purchased by the Dutch in the 1600's. It was later acquired by the British provincial government and made the Manor of Fordham. An early deed described the property as: "situate upon the main continent lying to the eastward of the Harlem River near unto ye passage commonly called Spiting Devil, upon which ye new Dorp or village is erected, known by the name of Fordham."

"Fordham" is derived from the Anglo Saxon words "ford" meaning to wade across a body of water, and "ham" meaning

Photo: Fordham Archives

The Rose Hill estate's "Main Building," the center of which is the original part of today's Administration Building, as it looked in the 1800's.

house or home. Hence, a wading place by a settlement. The name of the college would not be changed officially to Fordham University until 1907.

In 1678, John Archer, the Lord of the Manor who was known as the John Jacob Astor of the 17th century, sold 102 acres of farmland to Roger Barton, another Englishman. In 1694, upon Barton's death, it was subdivided. The southern half, roughly today's Fordham campus, was sold to a Dutchman named Reyer Michielsen. It was later passed on to his son-in-law, Benjamin Corsa who acquired additional property, extending the parcel to the Bronx River.

Corsa was the grandfather of Andrew Corsa, a Revolutionary War hero believed to have been born in the property's manor house at the approximate site of today's Collins Hall. (The young Andrew fought for the revolution, while his father, Isaac, remained on the side of the British crown, which eventually branded him a traitor.)

In 1786, after the war ended, the Corsas were no longer in a position to retain the property. It became home to a creditor, Robert Watts and his wife, Lady Mary Alexander. She was the daughter of General William Alexander, Lord Stirling, an aide to General George Washington. Watts named the property Rose Hill after his family home back in Scotland. Eight sales later it ended up in the hands of Andrew Carrigan, a wealthy merchant, who sold it to Archbishop Hughes on August 29, 1839.

Hughes, born in 1797 at Annaloghan near Augher, County Tyrone, Ireland, was a larger than life character who came to the U.S. intent on becoming a priest, despite an array of obstacles. At one point he was even confused with another priest and denied an assignment, which led many to believe his ascendancy to be leader of the Catholic Church in New York was divine intervention. This was the man who erected St. Patrick's Cathedral on Fifth Avenue after the church outgrew the previous St. Patrick's on Mott Street in lower Manhattan. In 1847, he was even singled out by former President John Quincy Adams, then a Congressman from Massachusetts, to preach before Congress at the Capitol in Washington. The text he chose: "Christianity, the Only Source of Moral, Social and Political Regeneration."

Surly and demanding, Hughes was nicknamed "Dagger John" for his aggressiveness and his habit of signing his name with a dagger-like cross. (Fordham grads from the 70's and 80's will remember the bar close to campus named Dagger John's, a paean to the founder, and there is a current on-campus spot with the same name.) Orestes Brownson, editor of Brownson's Quarterly Review and a leading thinker of the time, quoted Hughes as saying, "I will suffer no man in my diocese that I cannot control. I will either put him down, or he shall put me down." (Brownson was a regular speaker at St. John's College who received an honorary degree in 1850. A bronze statue of his likeness still resides in the space bordered by Queens Court, the church and Collins Auditorium.)

When Hughes was appointed prelate of the church in New York, he was intent on expanding its reach to meet the needs of a growing Catholic population. Indeed, he had a mandate from Pope Gregory XVI. There were too few priests and few actual churches – parishioners had to travel long distances to worship – and there was very little Catholic education. Hughes was determined to change that, and he did. Hundreds of new churches were built under his tutelage and he established a number of schools and hospitals.

The Archbishop was resolute about the need for Catholic schools out of his near obsession over the bias against Catholics in the public schools of his era. According to Thomas Gaffney Taaffe's aforementioned book, the Public School Society, a private corporation that managed the schools, "disbursed the funds provided by the city for the maintenance of the schools, chose the books to be used and regulated the entire working of the system. The textbooks used teemed with the usual falsehood and calumnies against Catholicity. The instructors were thoroughly imbued with the anti-Catholic spirit of the age and the city schools were practically turned into proselytizing institutions of the most flagrant kind."

"Though the society received state funding, it was essentially a private Protestant organization that taught Protestantism and used the Protestant Bible. Worse, from Hughes's point of view, it had pupils read such books as *The Irish Heart*, which taught that 'the emigration from Ireland to America of annually increasing numbers, extremely needy, and in many cases drunken and depraved, has become a subject for all our grave and fearful reflection,'" wrote William J. Stern in a 1997 *City Journal* article entitled "How Dagger John Saved New York's Irish." Stern reported that Hughes (with the support of New York's 12,000 Jews) wanted an end to such sectarian education, and he desired, above all, state aid for Catholic schools, just as the state had funded denominational schools before 1826. The outcome of the struggle pleased few: the Maclay Bill of 1842 barred all religious instruction from public schools and provided no state money to denominational schools. On the night the bill was passed, a mob ransacked Hughes' residence and the authorities had to call out the militia to protect the city's Catholic churches.

Hughes fought his battle in the press, in speeches and even with the state legislature and was able to have the society overthrown through his relationship with then Mayor Robert H. Morris. He was active in the fight against the famous Know-Nothing movement and influenced Mayor Morris to use the police force to quell the group. Hughes warned, "If a single Catholic Church were burned in New York, the city would become a second Moscow."

The Know-Nothing was a political society made up of the Protestant political faction of the 1850s, characterized by political xenophobia, anti-Catholic sentiment, and occasional bouts of violence. It was empowered by popular fears that the country was being overwhelmed by German and Irish Catholic immigrants believed to be under the control of the Pope, and was intent on stopping immigration. The origin of the "Know-Nothing" term came from the semi-secret nature of the party.

When a member was asked about its activities, he was supposed to reply, "I Know-Nothing."

St. John's College was actually the first Catholic college in the U.S., north of Georgetown. Hughes went to great lengths to fulfill his (and the Pope's) vision and to fight the anti-Catholic sentiment of the time. He wanted to educate wealthy young Catholic men

Rodrigue's Coffee House, one of the earliest buildings on campus, was home to the university architect and Archbishop Hughes' brother-in-law.

and to remove them from the influence of the Protestants, who would otherwise have taken control of their young minds, as he saw it.

To procure the capital needed to purchase the land and make accommodations for the school, he raised donations from wealthy Catholics in and around New York City and even traveled to Europe on a solicitation junket. Part of the money was borrowed at five percent interest. Whether by luck or by design in choosing the location, the Harlem Railroad was being expanded to reach Fordham at the time. The station was opened in October 1841 with a grey stone depot just adjacent to the campus. (When the archbishop ceded a right-of-way off the western edge of the property to the railroad, he was given one dollar and two tickets per year in perpetuity for the college president. Even more important than the tickets, he was able to make sure the tracks didn't run right through his land, which was the original plan.)

8

Hughes chose his own 44th birthday and the Saint Day of his namesake (and that of the college) as the day the school was founded, St. John the Baptist Day, June 24, 1841. There were six students, all male, and 10 professors, though the various accounts available offer conflicting numbers. The curriculum consisted of rhetoric (speech/elocution), belles-letteres (humanities), Greek, mathematics, moral philosophy, Hebrew, Latin, physics, chemistry, Spanish, German, French and Christian doctrine. One of the first students was Rev. Patrick F. Dealy, later president of the college, whose namesake building stands today at the edge of Edward's Parade.

The only women on campus at the time were female servants and a contingent of Sisters of Charity who managed the infirmary, wardrobe and kitchen. They also looked after the youngest group of boys.

St. John's first president was Rev. John McCloskey, eventually the first American cardinal and the next Archbishop of New York. In five successive years, there would be four presidents, including Rev. James Roosevelt Bayley, a distant cousin of Presidents Theodore and Franklin D. Roosevelt and the nephew of Elizabeth Ann Seton, the first female American saint. He would later be Archbishop of Baltimore.

At the time of its founding, the campus had just a few structures, the oldest of which was the original manor house. The building was said to have been used by General George Washington as a headquarters during his many travels between New York City and upstate New York during the Revolutionary War. However, the only written evidence available indicates that Washington and his men simply stopped at the property's gate to pick up Andrew Corsa who was their guide about the area. The wooden structure was also known in lore to be the principal setting of James Fenimore Cooper's novel, *The Spy*. The building, a two-story center hall home, with adjoining east and west wings and porches at the end of each, was torn down in 1896 to the dismay of many.

There was also what was first known as the "main building," the center portion of today's stone Administration Building, built by Horatio Shephard Moat, an English-born physician and herbalist from Brooklyn, in 1838. Two one-story wings, much larger than the present two that replaced them in 1869, were added early on. Also surviving today are the white marble front portico and the fieldstone façade of the central portion.

As built, the main part of the house had a center hall and a staircase. To the north was a parlor, and to the south was a small chapel. The second floor was originally used for classrooms and had a small library, but later the Sodality Chapel was built there. The third floor had a dormitory for Jesuit brothers. On the roof was a white octagonal cupola used as an astronomical observatory. Moat's original northern wing was used as the student refectory, while the south wing became a study hall and then a student chapel. Attached to the end of the southern wing was a one story brick building that had a square three-story brick structure nicknamed "The Castle." It had a music room, reading room and offices.

"It was here," said Father Dealy many years later, "I made my first speech in 1843 on the occasion of a reception given by Bishop Hughes to several bishops and other prelates."

Beyond the buildings, there were expansive lawns, farmland, rustic lanes and patches of forest, described in almost every text that exists as idyllic. The greater manor was known to have had three taverns, two stores, a Dutch Reform Church and 30 or 40 homes scattered about its hilly terrain, according to Robert Bolton's *History of Westchester County* in 1848. There were two roads near the college. One was formed by today's Kingsbridge Road to the north as it joins East Tremont Road to the South. It ran from West Farms to Manhattan. The other would have been today's Fordham Road that began at Fordham Landing on the Harlem River and ended near the college.

The site of Keating Hall was a wooded hill. Beyond that, where today's parking lots exist, there was a low-lying marsh, which was flooded before each winter and used for skating and ice production.

By 1846, the school had two more buildings, both magnificent and both also still standing in 2013. Archbishop Hughes hired his brother-in-law, William Rodrigue, as an architect (also professor of drawing, penmanship and civil engineering), and provided him with quarters at the college. Rodrigue, married to Hughes' sister, Margaret, constructed a tiny cottage for his family in 1840. Once known as Alumni House, it is now Rodrigue's coffee house and was landmarked in 1981. Rodrigue is known to have opened a small quarry, somewhere near today's Freeman Hall, and then set out to build two outstanding structures.

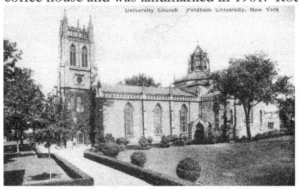

Photo: Fordham Archives

The original church did not have the spires or the dome. It has undergone significant change over the years.

Our Lady of Mercy Church, today's University Church, is now a Gothic structure with frescoed arches and ceilings. It was originally a good deal smaller with just a nave and a pointed steeple. Listed on the National Register of Historic Places, it was built in 1845 with stone from the site's quarry. The church has six windows representing the four evangelists, and Saints Peter and Paul, which were originally intended for St. Patrick's Cathedral. They were a gift from King Louis Philippe of France and were fabricated in Saint-Omer

11

during the early revival of stained glass art in France. (The windows didn't fit at St. Pat's, so Hughes had them installed at Fordham.) By the late 19th century, photographs show the original steeple had been replaced by a more substantial tower.

Over the first few decades, people from the surrounding Fordham Manor worshipped at the church with the Jesuits presiding, but in December 1893, the congregation moved to new quarters on Webster Avenue. Students rarely used the church, as the college chapel was located in the southern wing of the Administration Building. The church's front lawn, however, was the site of the earliest college commencements.

In the 1940's, the old altar was replaced by the 1879 original from St. Patrick's Cathedral, a rather serendipitous gift. Father Robert Gannon, then president, was riding in a car with his good friend, Cardinal Francis Spellman, who mentioned that the Cathedral was getting a new altar. "What are you doing with the old one,?" Gannon replied. At once, Fordham's chapel had a new and storied edifice.

After World War II, when the university decided to commemorate the more than 200 students who had died in the fighting, and because the church was in need of repair, a decision was made to rehab the building and to make the whole structure a memorial to those soldiers, at a cost of $200,000. Individual portions, such as the Stations of the Cross, were dedicated to alumni who served and died. The dedication took place on December 8, 1949, the day

Photo: Fordham Archives

12

after the eighth anniversary of Pearl Harbor.

The church underwent significant interior renovations in 1929, 1990 and 2004. Its most recent facelift was in 2013 when the organ loft was rehabbed and a new organ was dedicated. The 2004 project took 14 months and included comprehensive exterior restoration. Crews re-pointed the entire building, treated the marble stonework to prevent further deterioration, replaced exterior woodwork and restored windows in the nave. A pleasant surprise was uncovered when the deteriorating brownstone was removed from the entryway. Underneath was the original detail work featuring an inlaid stone pattern around the door. Using the original stone as a mold, workers recreated the pattern for the renovated entryway. The University Church was declared a New York City landmark in 1970, as were the Administration Building and St. John's Hall.

The second building erected by Archbishop Hughes was the Seminary of St. Joseph, now St. John's Hall, one of the university's most impressive structures with a massive arched entrance, latticed windows and vine-covered outer walls. Originally, there was a fireplace in each room. It was the first home of the preparatory school and has undergone many incarnations preceding today's use as a dormitory, including the addition of St. Robert's and Bishops Halls, one at each side, the whole of which is now called Queens Court.

Other, smaller buildings popped up over the next few years. They included an icehouse and a series of low sheds housing a bakery, pie shop, wardrobe and washrooms. These extended eastward to the area now known as Edwards Parade. Because there was well water on site, a pump stood adjacent to the field. Servants would bring pails of cold water each morning so the students could wash.

A charter from the New York State legislature was granted in April 1846 giving St. John's College, the power to "confer such literary honours, degrees or diplomas as are usually granted by any university, college or seminary of learning in the United States." The college was then able to grant degrees in theology, law, medicine and arts, but the new designation belied the truth.

Hughes was not happy with the leadership he had chosen and went looking for substitutes. He found them in a group of Jesuits at St. Mary's College in Kentucky, who were failing so far from civilization. He convinced its elders to move their seminary to New York, eager to have them lead his institution and determined not to choose a leadership from the Baltimore Jesuits, then running Georgetown College; Hughes would not have St. John's be a stepsister to Georgetown. He was resolute that it be the leading Catholic college in the country, one deserving of the growing metropolis 10 miles to its south.

Hughes knew what he was doing by importing the Jesuits to save his brainchild. As written in Robert R. Rusk's *The Doctrines of the Great Educators, Revised,* the Jesuit schools, "with their pedagogical principles, comprised a large segment of European scholastic institutions. Their growth between 1548 and 1773 was phenomenal. From 1548, when the first Jesuit school was founded at Messina in Sicily, to 1556, when Ignatius of Loyola, the Jesuit founder and general, died, 33 schools had been opened and six more were ready to open. The schools were located in Sicily, Italy, Spain, Portugal, Austria, Bohemia, France and Germany. By 1581 the number of schools increased to 150. When the official Ratio Studiorum (the Jesuit doctrine) of 1599 was promulgated, there were 245 schools. This number rose to 441 in 1626 to 669 in 1749. At the latter date in France alone there were 92 schools enrolling some 40,000 pupils. Meanwhile, the Jesuit system had spread from Europe to India, Cuba, Mexico and the Philippines."

Jesuit schools in France, Portugal, Germany and Italy at the time had up to 1,500 students. During these years of growth in the number of schools, enrollment also increased sharply. Jesuit schools in smaller towns averaged between 500 and 800, in the cities between 800 and 1,500. The majority were secondary schools, but a good many of them gradually added humanities and rhetoric, making them equivalent to the modern colleges of arts and sciences. At that time there were few Jesuit universities and four of note, Gandia and Coimbra in Spain, founded in 1549 and 1551, respectively, the Roman College, founded in 1551, and the French University of Pont-a-Mousson founded in 1575.

Many graduates of these schools distinguished themselves in literature, science, mathematics and the professions. There were: Corneille, the tragedian; Descartes, the philosopher and mathematician; Bossuet and Bourdaloue, the orators; Moliere, the comedian; d'Urfè, the romantic novelist; Monesquieu, the political philosopher, and Voltaire, the philosopher and critic, who was not a favorite of the Jesuits, but who was nevertheless a recipient of their training. Others were: Goldone, the creator of modern Italian comedy; Torquato Tass, the Italian poet and author of *Jerusalem Delivered*, and Calderon de la Barca, the Spanish dramatist and poet.

In June 1846, Bishop Hughes deeded the college to the 28 Jesuits who had made the arduous 10-day trip from Kentucky (via boat, stagecoach and train), but retained title to the seminary property, about nine acres, in return for a $40,000 mortgage (his original investment returned with 5% interest). He entrusted his namesake school to another strong figure who would shepherd the young institution in his vision, that of a leading college for young Catholic men. The first Jesuit president was the Rev. Augustus Thébaud, one of the Kentucky trekkers, who made an indelible mark.

What Father Thébaud and his colleagues found, according to the diary of a teacher, Father Michael Nash, were "without exception the worst boys I had ever met. Wild boys, and reckless boys I had met in St. Joseph's and St. Mary's Colleges, and in the schools of Louisville, but they were also gentlemen, sons of families of standing in society. Those of whom I had now charge, especially the N. York and Brooklyn boys, did not possess the remotest instinct of gentlemen."

In a pastoral letter, Archbishop Hughes wrote in 1846: "In five short years, St. John's College rose from the condition of an unfinished house in a field to the cluster of buildings of which it is now composed; and from an obscure Catholic school, beginning with six students, to the rank and privileges of a university. We deem it an evidence of Almighty God's approval that a numerous, learned and pious community of the illustrious Society of Jesus – a society especially instituted for the imparting of a high order of Christian education to youth – should have been found willing to take charge of it permanently."

Even though Hughes had relinquished control of the college, the diocesan seminary (and nine acres) remained in his hands for a few years, leading to lingering disputes over the property and finances. Hughes did not like the fact that others were in charge of what was originally his turf and at one point tried to appoint a secular priest to head the seminary. The Jesuits called that "intolerable" and also felt the property and buildings were not properly cared for. There were accusations that Jesuits were getting sick because the seminary's living conditions were below par, leading to sickness and even death among students and seminarians. The animosity between the factions would remain for decades.

At one point, tension between Archbishop Hughes and the Jesuits rose so high that the Vatican was called in. The Pope dispatched mediators in the form of two priests from the Maryland Province to smooth things over. In 1859, the seminary was moved to Troy, New York and the Jesuits took complete control of Rose Hill. The rest of the property was deeded to them in 1860. (During the years leading up to this schism, the name William Rodrigue, Hughes' brother-in-law, disappears from all official college catalogues; his job was likely a casualty of the dispute.)

Born in Nantes, France in 1807, Father Thébaud became a prominent force at the tiny college and beyond. Having entered the Society of Jesus in Italy, Thébaud was the son of a merchant during the dark days of the Reign of Terror. The elder Thébaud was somehow able to give his children the best religious education France had to offer at the time. His son studied science at the Sorbonne under Andre-Marie Ampére, the famous French physicist and mathematician, and other distinguished professors. He arrived in the U.S. in 1838, and became a chemistry teacher. He also earned a reputation as a Greek scholar before being attracted to New York by Archbishop Hughes.

President of St. John's from 1846 to 1851 and again from 1860 to 1863, Father Thébaud, 39 years old at the time of his installation, was the author of a series of books on religious and historic subjects and published numerous articles in the *Catholic World* and the *Catholic Quarterly Review*, two novels, *Louisa Kirkbridge, A Tale of New York* (1879), and *Twit Twats, An Allegorical Story of Birds* (1881). His more important works are: *The Irish Race in the Past and in the Present* (1873); *The Church and the Gentile World* (2 vols., 1878) and *The Church and the Moral World* (1881). From 1875 to his death, he also prepared his reminiscences in three volumes. Of these, the United States Catholic Historical Society published volume III (1904), giving an account of his American experiences, and volume I (1911), containing the recollections of his life in France.

During Father Thébaud's tenure, there was a great French influence and strong discipline. It cost $200 per year to attend St. John's, which included tuition and board; it was an extra $15 for students who stayed through the summer. (The average yearly wage in the U.S. before the Civil War was $300 per year, so we can assume that most of the students came from wealthy

17

families.) Students were further required to bring with them three suits for summer and three for winter, six shirts, six pairs of stockings, six pocket-handkerchiefs, six towels, three pairs of shoes or boots, a hat, cloak or overcoat, a silver spoon and silver drinking cup marked with his name. Wealthy indeed!

Students made extensive use of the expansive grounds, which at the time extended to the Bronx River. There was swimming, fishing, skating, tobogganing, handball, cricket and "rounders" or baseball, though not yet organized.

In addition to the library he established in 1850, Father Thébaud oversaw the opening of Fordham's first school in Manhattan, which became the independently chartered College of St. Francis Xavier in 1861.

It was in 1847 that Edgar Allan Poe arrived in the village of Fordham and began a friendship with the Jesuits, most notably Father Edward Doucet

Poe Cottage in the shadow of Rose Hill.

who went on to become president of the college. Poe would often take long walks from his cottage in the Kingsbridge section to Fordham to commune with nature and with the priests who befriended him. Just before his death in 1849, the poet, a man known for his depression, at least partially due to the tragic death of his young wife, published his famed work *The Bells*. Some credit the bells of Fordham's University Church as the inspiration for the poem – he could certainly hear them from his home on windy days – though the origin of the poem is disputed.

"I knew him well," said Father Doucet. "To bearing and countenance he was extremely refined. His features were

18

somewhat sharp and very thoughtful. He was well informed on all matters. I always thought he was a gentleman by nature and instinct."

On June 15, 1847, the first commencement was held. The *New York Herald* reported the following day:

"The first annual Commencement of this newly incorporated college took place at Fordham yesterday afternoon. All the regular trains of cars on the Harlem Railroad were crowded during the morning at 1 o'clock an extra train of six cars was dispatched to take up passengers, whose business or other engagements kept them in the city until that hour.

"The exercises were conducted in a large tent, erected for the occasion on the beautiful lawn in front of the college buildings, where, after the passengers from the last train had taken their places, there were present about two thousand persons, among whom we observed members of the city legislature, officers of the army, and other pubic persons, besides hundreds of pretty girls, beautiful young ladies and good-looking matrons.

"On the stage were seated Bishop Hughes, Bishop McCloskey [the first president], Joseph R. Chandler, Esq. of Philadelphia, Rev. Mr. Starrs, Rev. Mr. Bayley, Rev. Mr. C. Loudon, Canada, and Rev. Messrs. McCarron, O'Neil, McLellan, of this city, and the faculty of the college – Father Augustus J. Thébaud, President; Father John Larkin,

Photos: St. Francis Xavier (inset) and Fordham Archives

Father John Larkin and Larkin Hall.

19

Vice-President; Father William S. Murphy, Father Charles De Luynes, Father Louis Petit and Father H. du Merle.

"There were only four graduates, upon whom devolved the duty of delivering the orations, of which one was a discourse on Russia, by Mr. Charles De Bull. It was a credible performance, showing considerable historical knowledge and a happy turn of thought – reflection based on occurrences.

"The next oration was a Latin performance, *De Laudibus Linguae Lat. Oratio*, by P. McGovern who articulated clearly, and acquitted himself in all respects well, in a Latin speech of considerable length.

"The third was a discourse on O'Connell, by P. McCarron, who, with a modest introduction prefaced some quite eloquent remarks in laudation of the lamented Irish statesman.

"A discourse on 'Chivalry,' a good composition was delivered by Mr. Andrew J. Smith, who was also the honored graduate who delivered the Valedictory Address.

"The last discourse was of course the best, and was in consequence reserved till the last. It was written and delivered by Mr. S.H. Rosecrans, whose father is now Professor of Civil Engineering at West Point. It was entitled "Nothing Original."

Father Larkin spoke as well, telling the graduates:

"Gentlemen, let me impress upon your minds that, by asking for and receiving the academic honors, you enter into a solemn and public engagement to show yourselves worthy of the distinction which is conferred on you. This distinction is conferred upon you, not in our name, but in the name and by the authority of the Republic, and to the Republic both we and you are responsible. If the Republic invests us with a discretionary power to decorate with these distinctions those whom we judge worthy, it expects, and it has a right to expect, that they should show themselves on all occasions, in word and deed, friends of law and order, defenders of truth and justice, supporters of sound morality.

"Receive your diploma and Bachelor of Arts, and remember the engagements which you contract."

Father Larkin, born in Durham, England, educated in Paris, and Montreal and one of the Jesuits from Kentucky, rose from the vice presidency to the presidency in 1851. A man who arrived at Fordham with a reputation of his own, Larkin had been dispatched by his superiors to found the Church of St. Francis Xavier, still a New York City edifice in 2013, on West 16th Street. He was known as an orator and proved himself to be a respected and beloved leader at Fordham. A building in his name stands today as well. Larkin was described as one of the most handsome and most erudite men Fordham had seen.

"No man," said the journalist John R. G. Hassard, a former student, "who was at St. John's between 1851 and 1854 can speak of Father John Larkin without a quickening pulse. For me, ever since I first saw him 35 years ago, the college has been filled with his majestic presence." Hassard went on to describe the priest as a "Greek god."

The new president made his mark as an inspirational leader and his work to beef up the curriculum. It became required that students be proficient in the Greek and Latin classics and that they pass stringent exams in algebra, geometry and trigonometry. The course of study was henceforth modeled on the Jesuit Ratio Studiorum that dates back to 1599.

In Robert R. Rusk's 1957 book, *The Doctrines of the Great Educators*, he outlines the eight contributions made by the Jesuits to educational theory, based on the famous Ratio document.

"First, a uniform and universal method. Second, Jesuit teachers, far from being subordinated to method, played a principal role in the system and were thoroughly trained for it. Third, though from the beginning the Latin and Greek classics were predominant in the curriculum, the use of the mother tongue, the principles of mathematics, and the methods of natural science, were given their proper place when they proved to be of permanent value. Fourth, in retaining the drama as an educational instrument, the Jesuits anticipated the modern movement represented by what is termed the dramatic method of teaching history. Fifth, in insisting on the speaking of Latin, they likewise anticipated the direct method of teaching the classics. Sixth, the Jesuits substituted supervision for compulsion and dissociated punishment from teaching. Seventh, by promoting abler students after only half a session in a grade, they introduced a procedure now adopted by a number of modern school systems. Eighth, in Sacramental Confession and Communion the Society possesses powerful instruments for the moral and religious education of the pupil."

While Larkin was undoubtedly popular among the young men on campus, he also presided over one of its first disputes. For some reason, he suspended the celebration of St. Patrick's Day, normally a huge day for the young, mostly Irish Catholic, students. Many interpreted Larkin's action as a slight, derived from his British blood and perceived prejudice.

A revolt was mounted by the students who hurled marbles at just about all the panes of glass on campus. A number of young men were expelled and some were forced to pay for each of the panes he had broken.

Accounts of the time explain that Irish students were particularly sensitive to their heritage since the potato famine, known as the "Great Hunger," (1845-49) was fresh in their minds. More than 100,000 Irish citizens had died. In fact, a number of Fordham Jesuits were dispatched to Montreal to tend to Irish refugees who fled there. Reports suggest Father Larkin was not anti-Irish, but we still don't know why he stood in the way of the St. Patrick's celebration that year.

Even more daunting than misbehaving students for Father Larkin was the continued threat from the Know-Nothings, a secondary result of the famine since there was suddenly a new influx of Irish immigrants in New York. They, like many immigrant groups, were looked down upon by those who had already established themselves on America's shores. There was a great deal of bigotry that reached the Fordham neighborhood.

Reports of the time tell of at least two meetings of the Know-Nothing branch headquartered in Fordham Heights. The group tried to organize the burning of the college, though these efforts were put down after a great deal of negotiation. That didn't stop the tension. The priests of St. John's were actually given muskets by the government so they could defend themselves and their young charges. No violence ever reached St. John's College, but the muskets remained and became legendary as props for the Drama Society for a number of years.

One of the few *genuine* faults attributed to Father Larkin was his hatred of journalism and journalists. He tried to stop the founding of a school newspaper, though a publication called the *Goose-Quill* was established by three students (one of whom was the aforementioned John Hassard, '55) in 1853. They appointed an anonymous editor, likely the three founders, known by the singular name, "Ham." The *Goose-Quill* was a monthly that ran 28 to 30 pages. It was neither formally

Photo: Fordham Archives

The Goose-Quill was hand-written and posted, not reproduced.

23

printed nor distributed, but merely posted on large sheets of paper. It certainly did not travel beyond the confines of the school. Another of the *Goose-Quill* founders, the future U.S. Army General Martin T. McMahon, wrote:

"When the *Goose-Quill* was first established, it was rather ignored than permitted by the college authorities. We never, however, could obtain permission to print it. Father Larkin, under whose reign it came into being, was singularly conservative in some things, and never an admirer of newspapers. A favorite expression of his in the class-room when criticizing our compositions was: 'That is newspaper slang.' In fact, he forbade us to read in the newspapers any editorial articles and begged us merely to confine ourselves to the telegraph items of news."

By 1854, the presidency of Fordham was passed to yet another Jesuit, Rev. Remigius Tellier, an Italian who didn't build buildings, but he did add to life at Fordham significantly by initiating a baseball team, its first organized athletic organization, said to play the first official competition between two colleges in the U.S. – in any sport. Established on September 13, 1859, the team was known as the Rose Hill Base-ball Club (sic) and played its first game on November 3, 1859, against a team from St. Francis Xavier College. Rose Hill won, 33-11.

One of the team's early players was Estaban Bellan who went on to become the first Latin American major league baseball player. Bellan, a native of Cuba, played for the Troy Haymakers (later the New York Giants) after

Photo: Fordham Archives
An early baseball team in front of St. John's Hall.

graduating from Fordham. He eventually made his way back to his native country as a player and manager and is still celebrated in Cuba.

Father Tellier, the sixth president, also instituted semi-annual exams, in February and June, and was known for originating the St. John's Debating Society in 1854, limited to those students taking philosophy and rhetoric. (It is now the oldest club on campus, regularly placing among the top teams in the country.) The earliest members wore a gold badge in the shape of a shield with a Maltese cross at its center. It bore the Greek letters, Pi Phi Kappa Nu. The first topic was the Crimean War, the conflict then raging between the Russian Empire and an alliance of the French Empire, the British Empire, the Ottoman Empire and the Kingdom of Sardinia. The war was part of a long-running contest between major European powers for influence over territories of the declining Ottoman Empire. The young scholars were asked to debate the following: "Were the Western powers, as Christian nations, justified in espousing the cause of the Turks?"

Sadly, Father Tellier's tenure was also marked by the demise of the *Goose-Quill*. Though there were other attempts to revive journalism – with efforts known as *Sem*, *The Collegian* and *The Spy* - there would be no official newspaper at Fordham for another 20 years when *The Fordham Monthly* appeared. *The Ram*, a weekly, didn't debut until the early 20th century.

Theater was born at Fordham in 1855 with the dawn of the St. John's Dramatic Society. The first two student-staged productions were Shakespeare's *Henry IV* and *The Seven Clerks* by Thomas Egerton Wilks.

The pre-Civil War years at the young college were also known for very strong discipline, which included flogging and whipping by the Jesuits and outsiders hired specifically to be disciplinarians. Students marched quietly to prayers, study hall and meals. Parents could visit on Sunday afternoons. It is very possible that the lack of newspaper reporting and the fear students had of being beaten were intertwined.

A single teacher taught most of the liberal arts classes. The instructor got to know his students and their individual strengths and weaknesses, a boon to learning, and teachers had the same students for a year or two. Classes were supplemented by study halls, which supported the intense scholarly atmosphere that was also competitive.

Father Tellier retired in 1859 and was replaced in 1860 by the former president, Augustus Thébaud. During his second term, the college purchased the St. Joseph's seminary building (St. John's Hall) and the University Church from Archbishop Hughes for $85,000.

Thébaud made three additional purchases that would have long-lasting effects. He bought two stone quarries, one a marble quarry in the Tremont section of the Bronx and a second similar one on Bathgate Avenue closer to the college. They supplied the beautiful stone used to erect a number of buildings on the Fordham campus. He also purchased a neighboring property, Powell Farm, to the south of the original land.

Not surprisingly, a period of construction began. Father Thébaud undertook erection of a number of wooden buildings and the stone "gatekeeper's lodge" at Third Avenue and Fordham Road in 1862. Now known as Alpha House, it is home to the Honors Program and has since been moved to the center of campus.

The Gatekeeper's Lodge, now Alpha House.

He also laid out a number of pathways and lined them with trees, some of which remain.

Among the first graduates of St. John's College were numerous future priests, bishops, lawyers, judges and the future university president, Father Patrick Dealy. There was a prominent secessionist, Michael O'Connor of Charleston, South Carolina, who became a member of Congress after the Civil War. Other members of the early graduating classes who also reached distinction were: John La Farge, the painter; Ignatius Donnelly, the author; John R.G. Hassard, the journalist; Thomas B. Connery for many years editor-in-chief of the *New York Herald*; U.S. Army General James O'Beirne; Judges Morgan O'Brien and Henry H. Dodge, and many well-known lawyers: Anthony Hirst of Philadelphia, Philip van Dyke, and William B. Moran of Detroit, a member of the Supreme Court of Michigan; John A. Mooney of New York, a well-known writer; Ignatius and Thomas McManus, of Mexico, and Michael F. Dooley, of Providence, all bankers. Many students entered the clergy and reached positions of influence. Among them were Cardinal John Farley, Bishop Michael J. Hoban of Scranton, Bishop Sylvester H. Rosecrans of Columbus, Winand M. Wigger, Bishop of Newark, Monsignor Ernest Van Dyke of Detroit, Monsignor O'Connor of Charleston and Monsignors Lynch and Mooney, both of New York. There were also numerous Jesuit priests.

As noted, John Rose Greene Hassard went on to become a famous New York City newspaperman and historian. Born in 1836, his parents were Episcopalians. His mother was the granddaughter of Commodore James Nicholson, a legendary officer in the Continental Navy during the Revolutionary War whose family was renowned in American naval history. (Commodore Nicholson aided General Washington's forces during the Battle of Trenton.) Hassard became a Catholic at the age of 15 and, after graduation from St. John's, entered the diocesan seminary determined to become a priest, but poor health got in his way and he turned to writing.

Hassard was the first editor of *Catholic World Magazine* and had jobs as assistant editor of the *Chicago Republican* and the *American Cyclopedia*. He eventually joined the editorial staff of the *New York Tribune* and was mainly the literary and musical critic. According to the *Catholic Encyclopedia*, "his critical judgment and cultivated taste did much for the advancement of the highest musical art. He had a peculiarly impartial mind, and in his writings displayed a remarkable purity of style and vigour of expression." In addition to his work as a journalist, Hassard wrote a well-regarded book on the life of Archbishop Hughes and a short one on that of Pope Pius IX. He also wrote a *History of the United States* in both extended and abridged forms for use in Catholic colleges and schools.

During this time in U.S. history, Abraham Lincoln was just about to run for president and visited New York to make his famous speech at Cooper Union. It is considered one of his most important orations and some have believed it was responsible for making him president. In it, Lincoln laid out his views on slavery, affirming that he did not wish it to be expanded into the western territories and claiming that the Founding Fathers would agree with this position. John Hassard's *New York Tribune* (founded by Horace Greeley) hailed it as "one of the happiest and most convincing political arguments ever made in this City...No man ever made such an impression on his first appeal to a New-York audience."

A few miles north, St. John's College was in a strong position with 200 students, but the Civil War would change that.

Chapter II:
Fordham and the Civil War

Unlike Georgetown whose campus housed a military hospital, the Civil War did not interrupt the bucolic atmosphere at Rose Hill, but the bloody conflict did have an influence on St. John's College and vice versa. There was a drop in the student population during the great conflict that would claim the lives of at

Photo: Fordham Archives

St. John's College students around the time of the Civil War.

least 620,000 Americans, including a number of men from Fordham.

There was no official Jesuit position on the war and students at St. John's were forbidden from taking sides in arguments on the topic. There is, however, evidence that the Jesuits were at least somewhat tolerant of slavery. In Father Thébaud's autobiography, he wrote that Catholic slave owners treated their slaves with respect and their slaves were happy. He was not an abolitionist, but he claimed to be in favor of the Emancipation Proclamation. Thébaud said he wished the emancipation had come when the church was prepared to bring the freed Negroes into Christianity.

"If, at the time of the emancipation of the slaves by Lincoln, there had been in the South priests enough to take care of the colored population, there would be at this moment a large number of parishes mainly composed of colored people. Unfortunately the decree of emancipation came too suddenly; nobody was prepared for such a sweeping measure; and it is now difficult to gather the scattered sheep who took to their heels as soon as they heard they were free," he wrote in 1904. Since the Jesuits had land in the South, it is also believed they did not want to become enemies of Confederate President Jefferson Davis.

Archbishop Hughes, likewise, had written that slavery "was not an absolute and unmitigated evil," though he was sent to Europe by President Lincoln to drum up support for the Union.

According to Father Gannon's *Up to the Present: The Story of Fordham*, four Fordham alumni were generals in the Union Army. Seven were colonels and seven were captains. Eight alumni served with the Confederates, as many St. John's students were originally from southern states.

Among those Confederate soldiers were members of the Pinckney family of Pinckney Colony, South Carolina who were considered some of the state's founding fathers. They were plantation owners and rice planters whose ancestors were part of the Constitutional Convention. Three sons of this family, William (1831-1855), Eustace Bellinger (1835-1925) and Charles (1833-Unknown) attended St. John's College in the 1850's. The latter two served with the South under General Robert E. Lee.

The library of the University of South Carolina has two letters to Eustace from a St. John's classmate, P.K. Molony. Recalling his college experiences on October 18, 1852, Molony expressed some regret: "I did not know how pleasant college life was, until it had passed" and told Pinckney, who left college after the Christmas holidays in 1952, "you had a happier life *there*, than you ever will elsewhere." On January 14, 1853, Molony wrote that he hoped "you did not leave it in disgust as a great many of your friends have." Another classmate, Richard Stevenson, asked on January 11th of that year if Pinckney departed St. John's to attend college in France and recounted a campus tussle. "How the chairs and cups did fly; it was fun to see them light on Bidwell's head." While at St. John's, Eustace Pinckney received several notes written on lace-edged stationery from his cousin and childhood sweetheart, Mary Augusta Bellinger.

During the war, there were also a number of Jesuit priests who left the safety of New York to become chaplains on the bloody battlefields and some of the younger students volunteered as drummer boys. We know that at least two St. John's students lost their lives and more than one went on to win the military's highest honor, the Medal of Honor. One notable St. John's student headed a regiment of Black soldiers.

Union General Martin Thomas McMahon, class of 1855, co-founder of the first "newspaper" at Fordham, the *Goose-Quill*, and a founding member of the debating society, is likely the most prominent graduate of the Civil War era. General McMahon, who went on to become a judge in New York City, was one of three brothers, all St. John's College men, who became lawyers

and gave up their law practices to fight. The two older siblings, Colonel James Power McMahon (1836-1864) and Colonel John Eugene McMahon (1834-1863), were commanders of the 14th New York Volunteer Infantry Regiment. Both died during the war – John, class of 1852, from disease, and James from injuries sustained at the Battle of Cold Harbor, Virginia, one of General Ulysses S. Grant's final battles. Ironically, James had survived the war's bloodiest battle at Antietam.

General Martin Thomas McMahon in a photo taken by Matthew Brady.

General McMahon was initially a captain and headed a cavalry unit, but that wasn't good enough for him. When he was told that his company would not go to the front lines, he quit and went back east where he was eventually named aide-de-camp to General George McClellan in the Army of the Potomac. His actual rank was Brevet Major General and he won the Medal of Honor fighting in the Battle of White Oak Swamp, Virginia on June 30, 1862, when he was 24 years old. The citation, conferred years later in 1891, read "Under fire of the enemy, successfully destroyed a valuable train that had been abandoned and prevented it from falling into the hands of the enemy."

McMahon, born in Canada but raised in New York City, graduated from St. John's in 1855 and then studied law in Buffalo, receiving his Master's degree in 1857. He later went west and worked as a special agent for the post office in California where he was admitted to the Sacramento, California bar in 1861.

Following the war, McMahon became a person of some renown in New York City and throughout the state. After resigning his Army commission he returned to Fordham to earn a Doctor of Laws from St. John's College. He served as New York City's corporation counsel for two years before becoming the United States minister to Paraguay, a position he held from 1868 to 1869. After returning to the U.S., he served as the Receiver of Taxes in New York and then worked as a U.S. Marshal. During the 1880's he became connected with the National Soldiers' Home and was its president for several years. General McMahon switched to politics and became a member of the New York State Assembly (New York Co., 7th D.) in 1891 and the State Senate from 1892 to 1895. A president of the St. John's College alumni association, he was elected a judge of the Court of General Sessions in 1896, a position he held until his death on April 21, 1906, in Manhattan.

From General McMahon's obituary in *The New York Times*:

"Gen. Martin T. McMahon, Judge of the Court of General Sessions died in his apartments at the Grosvenor, Fifth Avenue and Tenth Street, last night, of pneumonia, after a day's illness.

"Gen. McMahon was one of the conspicuous figures of the Civil War. He served in the campaigns of the Army of the Potomac, was brevetted a Major General, and received the Congressional medal for bravery...He was born in Laprairie County, Quebec, Canada, on March 21, 1838. Early in life, Gen. McMahon came to New York where he received his education. He was graduated from St. John's College, Fordham, in 1855. He got his Master's degree in 1857 and his Alma Mater conferred the degree of Doctor of Laws upon him in 1866...Gen. McMahon had served on the General Sessions bench since 1896. His term would have expired on Dec. 31, 1909. He was a member of the Catholic, Manhattan, Army and Navy and Democratic Clubs, the Dunlap Society, the Liederkranz, the Military Order of the Loyal Legion, the Metropolitan Museum of Art, and the Society of the Army of the Potomac."

Another Fordham war hero was Colonel Robert Gould Shaw, famed commander of the all-Black 54th Massachusetts Volunteer Infantry American Civil War regiment. A bronze sculpture of him, by sculptor Augustus Saint-Gaudens and architect Stanford White, stands today in Boston Commons across from the Massachusetts State House. The regiment was one of the first official African American units in the United States, after the First South Carolina Volunteers (Union) Unit, made up of freed slaves. Many African Americans had been soldiers during the Revolution and the War of 1812, but there hadn't been an all-Black regiment until this time.

A former student at the St. John's College junior division, the forerunner of Fordham Preparatory School, Colonel Shaw is the soldier portrayed by Matthew Broderick in the 1989 movie, *Glory*. He died valiantly at the battle of Fort Wagner in South Carolina on July 18, 1863. The film was based on the book, *One Gallant*

Rush by Peter Burchard, a compilation of the 200-plus letters Shaw wrote to his friends and family during the war that reside today at Harvard's Houghton Library. (The movie also starred the Oscar-winning actor Denzel Washington, Fordham class of 1976, who played a defiant former slave.)

Shaw, born October 10, 1837 in Boston, to a prominent abolitionist family, was the son of Francis George and Sarah Blake (Sturgis) Shaw, Unitarian philanthropists. They had inherited the estate of Shaw's grandfather, also Robert Gould Shaw (1776-1853), a wealthy merchant. Young Shaw studied abroad in Switzerland, Italy, Norway and Sweden as a boy and was sent to St. John's College after the family landed on Staten Island in the early 1850's. After Fordham, Shaw went to Harvard University, but did not graduate.

Robert Gould Shaw

Upon President Lincoln's election and the war's outbreak, Shaw joined the 7th New York Militia, where he helped to defend the nation's capital in Washington, D.C. Soon after, he joined the 2nd Massachusetts Infantry as a second lieutenant and participated in the battles of Winchester, Cedar Mountain and Antietam.

Shaw's own father, Francis, approached his son about taking command of an all-Black regiment in late 1862 at the request of Massachusetts Governor John A. Andrew. According to his letters, the younger man was against it at first because he wasn't sure such a unit could succeed. But, he reconsidered.

In a letter to his then fiancée, Anna Kneeland Haggerty, he said he "had to prove that the Negro can be a good soldier."

Once in command of the group, Shaw was a full convert. He grew respectful of the soldiers in his unit and wrote that they impressed him. He went to bat for his men when he learned the Black soldiers were not being paid commensurate with their white counterparts. He was behind a boycott that would ultimately correct the inequality. The enlisted men of the 54th Massachusetts Infantry (and the sister 55th) refused pay until Congress granted them full back pay at the white pay rate in August 1864.

During early 1863, Shaw was promoted to Major, then to Colonel. In May, he married Haggerty (1835-1907) in New York City and they spent some time on Anna's family farm in Lennox, Massachusetts awaiting the 54th Infantry's deployment from Boston to Charleston, South Carolina, to attack the Confederate stronghold there.

As depicted by Broderick in *Glory*, on July 18, 1863, the 54th Infantry, with two brigades of white troops, attacked the Confederacy's Fort Wagner. Despite heavy fire from the opposition, Shaw prompted his men, shouting, "Forward, Fifty-Fourth, Forward!" He mounted a parapet, continuing his chant, but was shot in the heart and died almost immediately.

The Confederate soldiers, winners of the battle, buried Colonel Shaw in a mass grave with many of his men, which was intended as a slight. Later, it was reported that commanding Confederate General Johnson Hagood returned the bodies of the other Union officers who died at Fort Wagner, but left Shaw behind.

Hagood told a Union surgeon who was a prisoner of war, "Had he [Shaw] been in command of white troops, I should have given him an honorable burial; as it is, I shall bury him in the common trench with the negroes that fell with him." Shaw's family did try to locate his body after the war, but his father said publicly that he was proud that his son was interred with the troops in his command, that his burial was "befitting his role as a soldier and a crusader for social justice." In a letter to the regimental surgeon, Lincoln Stone, Frank Shaw wrote:

"We would not have his body removed from where it lies surrounded by his brave and devoted soldiers. We can imagine no holier place than that in which he lies, among his brave and devoted followers, nor wish for him better company – what a body-guard he has!"

Gen. James Rowan O'Beirne, yet another Fordham Civil War hero, also won the Medal of Honor. Born in Roscommon, Ireland, he was entrusted to the Jesuits by his parents when he was a young boy. O'Beirne trained briefly as a lawyer and entered the military as a private, rising through the ranks to Second Lieutenant, then to Brevet Brigadier-General. As an officer, he was a member of the 37th New York Regiment known as the "Irish Rifles" and served under Major General George B. McClellan. Seriously wounded in 1863 at the battle of Chancellorsville, O'Beirne was shot in the lung and leg and was hit in the head by a shell. He survived and was made Provost Marshal of Washington, D.C. in 1864.

His own writings tell us that he worked under Secretary of War Edward Stanton and was sent on special scouting missions, the most notable of which took place on the night of April 14, 1864 after President Lincoln was shot by John Wilkes Booth at Ford's Theater.

General James O'Beirne .

The New York Times wrote, "O'Beirne was officially in charge of the deathbed of President Lincoln and was the last of those engaged in that duty."

According to *The Irish in The American Civil War* by Damian Shiels, O'Beirne actually led the hunt for Booth, which has also been documented in numerous books and movies:

"After Booth had bolted on horseback from the Washington theatre on that Good Friday night, April 14,1865, Lincoln was rushed to a boarding house across the street, where he lay dying.

"O'Beirne escorted Vice President Andrew Johnston to the president's bedside, after the second in command had himself avoided a similar fate when his would-be-killer George Atzerodt lost his nerve at the crucial moment.

"Secretary of State William Seward wasn't so lucky after a simultaneous attack saw him receive multiple stab wounds at the hands of Lewis Powell.

"Merely days after Republican forces had restored the Union to end the American Civil War its top-brass had now received a damaging blow by Confederate sympathisers who, however late in the day, were intent on extracting their own pound of flesh.

"Secretary of War Edwin Stanton circled the wagons in the back room of the infamous boarding house and issued O'Beirne with orders that he was 'relieved from all other duty at this time, and directed to employ yourself and your detective force in the detection and arrest of the murderers of the President, and the assassins who attempted to murder Mr. Seward.'

"The Roscommon native (O'Beirne) had, at this stage, vast experience in the theatre of war. As captain of the 37th New York 'Irish Rifles' Infantry he was badly wounded by sniper fire to the chest, head and right leg at the 1863 Battle of Chancellorsville, on a day that was the second bloodiest in the entire American conflict.

"Acting on Stanton's instructions Major O'Beirne made his way through the capital's streets in the small hours of April 15.

He barged through the front doors of Kirkwood House, where Atzerodt had failed to go through with his orders. There O'Beirne discovered the room where the conspirator had been holed-up, and subsequently fled from. A loaded revolver was found under Atzerodt's bed pillow and a Bowie knife was also seized. These discoveries led directly to Atzerodt's arrest five days later at his cousin's house in Germantown, Maryland.

"O'Beirne's main quarry, though, was Booth. An actor by trade and an idealist, he was far from any villainous stereotype. The fugitive was noted at the time for being 'impossibly vain, preening, emotionally flamboyant, and possessed of raw talent and splendid élan.' With the help of a map of the upper Potomac that was picked up at Atzerodt's quarters, a goose chase ensued along its banks that lasted for 12 days, where Booth sheltered from his Roscommon hunter in a thicket of pine.

"When Booth crossed state boundaries into Virginia O'Beirne pinpointed him to the Garrett farm, a residence near the town of Bowling Green. The Major telegrammed Secretary Stanton, waiting for his cue to make a decisive move.

"Here, by all accounts, office politics took over and Stanton pulled the Kilrooskey native from the case. Much of the lucrative reward on offer was to go to a personal favourite of Stanton's Lafayette C. Baker.

"Along with his agents Baker finished the job Major O'Beirne had begun, smoking Booth out of a barn before he succumbed to gunfire. If O'Beirne's monetary reward of $2,500 was paltry when compared with the hand he played at a crucial time in American history, his achievements thereafter are notable only in their magnitude."

In letters, General O'Beirne's underscored the importance of the Fordham connection, even more than a century and a half ago, and tells of his attempts to help even Confederate former classmates, despite their obvious differences. This story is from a letter written by O'Beirne during the final days of the war, just prior to the assassination, when he was encamped within miles of the White House:

"It was here [during the Seven Days Battle on the Peninsula] that for the first time I met any of the Fordham boys who were serving in the Southern Army. Dillon of Georgia and Pinckney of South Carolina were among the number who were even then as conspicuous and notable as they were when at college in the football and athletic games. They had been taken prisoners I had heard, and learning where the fiery Dillon was, I decided to visit him and to take him something to eat because I knew that, on account of the long continued marching and quick changes, provisions had grown scarce and difficult to obtain. I had a lot of Irish stew made and with a couple of canteens of coffee I rode off from our camp to where the prisoners were.

"A steady, drizzling rain, which froze as it fell continuously during the night and morning rendered everyone cold and uncomfortable. Beneath a tree covered with icicles I found Dillon huddled among a group of Confederate soldiers with icicles hanging from their eyebrows and beards, trying to get warm by getting as near the conformation of human balls as possible. Saluting him cheerily as I jumped down from my horse and handling the coffee and edibles as carefully as possible, I offered them with as good grace as possible considering the forlorn condition of all covered with ice and wet as we were.

"Dillon stared at me with a blank look, without a word of reply and looked as haughty and unconscious of my presence as he could. He turned his fine and fiery red head aside to contemplate the cheerless scene from some other angle apparently and dismissed me from his thoughts. I had come on a long and unpleasant ride to look him up and help him, with much danger from a fugitive light-battery that opened on us at intervals, and here was my reward.

"I put the supplies down at his side, and smothering my indignant surprise, rode off to the Irish Brigade quarters nearby,

39

expecting to go to Mass there, as it was Sunday and called on Colonel Cavanaugh in his tent."

O'Beirne described running into yet another fellow Fordham man, though this one much younger than he, describing the boy as brave, but frightened. He said the boy was carrying a rifle that stopped working because it was clogged by sand and relayed telling the young man, "Throw it away and take the gun of one of these wounded soldiers and his ammunition, and commence firing. This he proceeded to do, and I never saw him afterwards, though I heard he had been wounded. I merely cite this as an illustration of the pluck of another Fordham boy under difficulties."

General O'Beirne went on to become an editor of the *Washington Gazette* and Washington correspondent for the *New York Herald*. On one assignment for the *Herald* during the Indian Wars, he was said to have ridden alongside the legendary General George Armstrong Custer. In the 1890's he worked at Ellis Island, watching over the throngs of Europeans arriving at America's shores. He also ran unsuccessfully for public office. When he died in 1917, at the age of 77 at his home at Manhattan's 352 West 117th Street, the Fordham Alumni Association was there to pay tribute alongside the Seventh Regiment Irish Rifles.

Among the even younger men from Rose Hill who went to war were a number of drummer boys. At least two were stationed in Florida with former professor, Father Michael Nash. Nash had enlisted as a chaplain with the Sixth Regiment Infantry known as "Wilson's Zouaves" after the unit commander, Colonel William Wilson, and the French army Zouaves who, like this particular unit, wore colorful uniforms. In a letter to Father Tellier back at Fordham, Father Nash reported losing his Mass kit in a Confederate raid on Camp Brown on the Gulf of Mexico's Santa Rosa Island and, like O'Beirne, described meeting former St. John's students:

"Frederick Goggins, our bold drummer-boy, sends his sincere regards to you and Father Legouais. He amuses me a great deal by his regrets for college life. 'If a boy does not like college, let him become a soldier, and he will see the happiness of a life he does not know to appreciate,' he remarked to me this morning. When we have anything severe on poor human nature to do or endure, for instance, to pass a dark foggy night in the trenches, he whispers to me: 'How would the Fordham boys like this?' Fred is a good boy and serves my Mass in turn with others, or at least did serve it, and I hope will again, when you will have sent a new chapelle to the 'army and flee of the gulf.'"

Father Nash was captured for a short time by the Confederates, but escaped when a fire broke out in the camp where he was being held.

Another drummer boy who made his way to Fordham after the war was Morgan J. O'Brien, who went on to become a "twirler" for the New York Mutuals (forerunner of baseball's

Yankees) and later a Justice of the Appellate Division of State Supreme Court in New York. Judge O'Brien later wrote:

Photo: Fordham Archives
Deal Hall with early members of the Cadet Corps.

"I was about 12 or 13 years of age, living with my parents on Sixth Street when the Civil War was being fought. One day while I was playing about the streets, the body of a little lad my own age, who had been killed while beating the drum for the G.A.R. [Grand Army of the Republic], was brought home to lie in state at the old Second Regiment on Seventh Street. He was given a great military funeral three days later. With visions of

41

saving the Union, I followed the march down Broadway to the Battery where the dead hero was placed aboard a ferry for burial in Brooklyn. Soon after, I ran away from home to go to war with a Regiment of Irish Riflemen of the Massachusetts Brigade."

O'Brien made it home and became a student at St. John's from whence he graduated in 1872.

As the story of Father Nash reveals, the soldiers from Fordham were not the only members of the community who went to war. There were many Jesuits who served as military chaplains.

One, Father Thomas Ouellet, ministered to the Sixty-Ninth New York Regiment. He was said to have "always found where the dying lay closest, where the danger was greatest, caring nothing for himself and endangering his life at every movement," according to Taaffe's book.

Of Father Nash, General McMahon was quoted as saying, "[he] did more to discipline Wilson's Zouaves than all of their officers."

Father Peter Tissot, later acting president of Fordham (1864-1865), is said to have attracted the attention of Brig. General Winfield S. Hancock for his chaplaincy at Antietam. His diaries, held in the Fordham University archives, reveal that he joined the "Irish Rifles" and spent at least two years ministering to the troops, including Fordham men he met along the way, hearing confessions and holding Mass. On one occasion, he mentioned running into a Fordham graduate, Major John Devereux of the 67th Pennsylvania regiment, class of 1848.

Tissot spent at least 17 days imprisoned by the Confederates in Richmond. He had been captured during a march because he was slowed down by illness. Of the conditions, he wrote of many long hikes in the cold and rain when the soldiers, carrying heavy loads would dispense with an item of clothing or a blanket, only to regret it later on.

Tissot's fascinating remembrances include an account of his induction in 1861. For his service, he was paid about $1400 per year, the equivalent of the salary for a "Captain of the Cavalry." He said he spent very little and kept no servant. "I paid a trifle to one of the men to take care of my horse when I had one." He lost at least one horse to a bullet during a barrage that missed him by inches in the Battle of Fair Oaks.

He also said, though he tried to avoid it, he ended up keeping the money of the men in his charge for safekeeping and also to send home to their families if they died, a task he carried out often enough. One night, he slept at the White House after dropping money off at the post office there.

One diary entry entered after the evacuation of Yorktown on May 3, 1862, truly demonstrates what was on the priest's mind at the time:

"Among those who passed me, one handed me his money, over one hundred dollars, to be sent to his mother. He was a poor fellow – an officer, who had been very pious in his younger days, but who had positively refused to go to confession. Time and again during winter, while we were in Camp Michigan, I had urged him to make his peace with God, but to no purpose. Finally one day I told him: "I have done my duty in regard to you. If anything happens to you; if you are killed and go to hell, you will have no one to blame but yourself." "That is true," he replied, "you have done your duty; I take the whole blame on myself." The day of the battle he seemed very sad, and said to some one that he thought he would surely be killed. And so he was, at the very beginning of the battle. I remember distinctly giving absolution when he was but a few paces ahead of me, after he handed me his money. If he was contrite then, he may have been pardoned in time."

Back on campus, the presidency of St. John's had changed hands once again with the installation of Rev. Edward Doucet, S.J., who numbered eighth in the order of presidents. Father

Doucet was known as a serious musician and strong preacher who had become a good friend to Edgar Allan Poe on his many jaunts to Fordham in earlier years. He served as president only from 1863-1865. There are conflicting reports; either he was ill or he was called away to Europe.

Father Doucet's successor was Rev. William Moylan, S.J. His major accomplishment is said to have been the construction of Senior Hall, or First Division building, the first of the structures built from the blue stone and marble of the stone quarries acquired by Father Thébaud. For many years, Senior Hall was the principal college building, a four-story structure with a mansard roof containing a gym, reading and billiard rooms, a study hall and dormitories for the oldest students. It is now the east wing of Dealy Hall. The western portion of this building was completed in 1891 for the 50th anniversary. In 1935 it was named for Father Patrick Dealy, president from 1882 to 1885.

Chapter III:
Reconstruction at Fordham

In the early 1850's there were 200 students at St. John's. There was a falling off at the time of the Civil War, but by the year 1869-70 there were 257 enrollees. After a phase of diminished attendance in the late 1870's – 327 in 1889 and 1890 – the number rose to 500 as the century came to a close.

The still small college, with a list of nine presidents by this time, celebrated its 25th anniversary in 1866 with a party for more than 2,000 people under a large tent on the grounds. It was just one year after the end of the Civil War and the shocking assassination of President Lincoln. The war had cost the north some $11 billion and the south $4 billion, to say nothing of the enormous loss of life and lifestyle.

William Marcy "Boss" Tweed was ruling New York City at the time. The city had been marred by draft riots that went on for five days. There was a great deal of poverty.

Once again, students were arriving from the southern part of the U.S. and from Latin America. According to archival records, 21 students had come from New Orleans alone. There were five foreign students – from England, France and Belgium. In 1869, there were a number of young men from Cuba. Tuition remained at $200 per year, but there were extra fees, $15 for washing and mending of clothing, $3 in physician's fees and $5 for the use of chemical apparatus. The fee to stay on campus over the summer was still $30.

The students continued to be treated rather harshly in terms of discipline. Beatings remained a consistent happenstance for those who veered from the rules and the strict code of conduct. Mass and prayers were a daily requirement. Letters from parents to students – and those written by the students to their parents – were censored. There would be no complaining that the food was terrible or that the conditions were harsh, but accounts indicate they were.

It's reported that the dormitories were still rather primitive. Rooms were cold; there was no running water. It wasn't unusual for a student to become seriously ill, or to die, as was the norm for this era. The young men were seldom allowed to leave campus on their own, but there were sporadic field trips – to the Jerome Park racetrack, to Manhattan or to swim in the Bronx River. All kinds of sports were played.

A farm on campus supplied meat from pigs and cattle. Located roughly in the vicinity of today's tennis courts, there were plowed fields and an orchard where apples, pears and cherries were grown. There was a small garden for vegetables such as tomatoes, potatoes and corn. A vineyard, near today's cemetery, produced grapes and wine. The food operation, which was said to have helped keep tuition costs down for decades, was run by Jesuit brothers who cultivated the crops and supervised the workers. The farm was removed in 1907, even though

This daily schedule comes from the *Rules and Customs Book* for St. John's College, Fordham, circa 1865:

A.M.
5:30 Rise, wash
6:00 Daily prayers & Mass
6:30 Study hall
7:30 Breakfast
8:00 Class
10:00 Recreation
10:15 Study Hall

P.M.
12:15 Dinner
12:45 Recreation
2:00 Study hall
3:00 Class
5:00 Recreation
5:30 Study hall
7:30 Supper
7:45 Recreation
8:15 Prayers & bed

it was said to be saving the school $1,000 per year.

Meals were made up of the following:

Breakfast: Hoecakes (fried cornmeal gruel), coffee and bread.

Supper: Hashed potatoes, beefsteak or another type of prepared meat, apple sauce, apples and grapes.

A light meal in between breakfast and supper was served at 4 p.m. Beverages served were typically ginger ale or sarsaparilla, and sometimes beer. For the Jesuits, many of whom were of European extraction, wine was naturally a staple.

On feast days and holidays, extra food and special desserts were permitted. Shellfish, including oysters, were considered treats. (Feast Days were many according to the Catholic calendar.) Talking during daytime meals was discouraged, except for grace. Eight men sat at a table, all facing forward toward a podium where most nights a student was chosen to read from one of the classics. In the evenings, after class, conversation was allowed.

During this era, some of Fordham's traditions were starting to take shape.

The university's official color, originally magenta, was changed to maroon when there was a rivalry with Harvard, which also boasted magenta (later changed to today's crimson). For a while, the two schools wore the same color during sporting events and the matter was supposed to have been settled by the outcome of a series of baseball games. Fordham won the games, but Harvard reneged on its promise. Both schools continued to use magenta until 1874 when the Fordham student government unanimously agreed to switch to maroon, not widely used at the time.

The ram became the Fordham mascot as a result of a cheer that Fordham fans sang during an 1893 football game against the United States Military Academy. The crowd began chanting, "One-damn, two-damn, three-damn, Ford-ham,!" which was an instant hit. Later, "damn" was sanitized to "ram" so the cheering would conform to the Jesuit image. Over the years, there would be at least 27 actual, living rams adopted as mascots. Many lost their lives to rival schools like Manhattan College, which took to kidnapping the poor ram, painting it or otherwise submitting it to torture. It was said that it took at least five men to bathe the 160-pound living rams and that they had voracious appetites, which is likely why a costumed student took over the mascot job in the cost conscious 1970's.

The Great Seal of Fordham University was designed to acknowledge the presence of the Society of Jesus. It bears the Greek letters of the lapidary form of Jesus Christ (IHS), with the cross at the center of the H and the three nails of the crucifixion beneath the epigraph. These figures, dressed in gold, lay in a field framed in maroon with silver fleur-de-lis at the edge, the flower being symbolic of the St. John's College French Jesuits of 1846. Above the central shield is the laurel crown, enclosing the university's disciplines: arts, science, philosophy, medicine and law. Below the shield is a blue scroll with the motto, Sapientia et Doctrina (wisdom and knowledge). In a circular maroon field embroidered with beads is Fordham's official name in Latin, Universitas Fordhamensis. At the field's lower edge is the founding year, 1841.

By 1868, Father Moylan, in office for just three years, was replaced by Rev. Joseph Shea, S.J., who served for six years. The student body at this time numbered 303, having fallen from 310 when Moylan took office. Southern Boulevard had just been built by the city, separating the main part of the campus from the vast acreage beyond the site of the future New York Botanical Gardens. By 1877, enrollment was just 166.

Shea, described as a gentle Canadian, tried changing the system of discipline at the college, making it more relaxed. By late in the century, students could sleep until six in the morning. In 1880, chairs replaced benches in the dining hall, then known as the refectory. Napkins were introduced, as were cups and saucers. Fire escapes and city water arrived in 1883.

Thomas J. A. Freeman, S.J., a renowned science professor.

Father Shea also hired a teacher revered for many years thereafter by students, Rev. Thomas J. A. Freeman. A graduate of the Columbia School of Mines, he was placed in charge of the science curriculum, which would soon grow. A building named after him remains today, adjacent to Thébaud and Dealy Halls, just at the edge of Edward's Parade. Father Freeman is noted for greatly improving the study of physics and chemistry, but also for a couple of close calls in the lab. There are reports that Freeman was present for two explosions. Once, he mistakenly mixed hydrogen and oxygen and was slightly injured. Another time, he and his assistant accidently set some paraffin on fire. The damage to the building extended to a number of frescos on the ceiling.

Notable students of the time were Rev. Charles F. H. O'Neill, '74, who became pastor of the Cathedral in Peoria, Illinois and chancellor of its diocese, and the formerly mentioned Morgan J.

O'Brien, '72, a New York State Supreme Court judge. Edward Bermudez, '74, later became a judge in New Orleans, while Joaquin Arrita, '71, went on to become secretary to the representative of San Salvador in the Pan-American Congress. John B. Shea, '74, served in the New York State Legislature. At least 135 of the first 521 St. John's graduates went on to the priesthood.

In 1874, Father Shea was succeeded by Rev. F. William Gockeln, a six foot two Prussian, who was noted as "one of the finest looking men in New York City." Shea's relaxation of the rules had been deemed a great failure, so Gockeln's first official act was to restore the strict discipline that had previously prevailed. He was said to have given notice that the rules would be strictly enforced.

Though a disciplinarian, Gockeln was called "a large-souled, big-hearted man" by one of his associates of the time, Father Patrick Halpin. Thomas Gaffney Taaffe said, "In spite of his radical policy and seemingly severe methods of government, the new rector soon found his way to the hearts of the students. He was a man well calculated to win the love, respect and admiration of all who came in contact with him. Genial and hearty, the soul of good-nature, scholarly, and with refinement and nobility stamped on every feature of his splendid face; he was indeed a man among men."

These years were considered down times for the college, partly due to the world at large. When enrollment reached 200 again in 1881, it was seen as a great victory. Writing a number of years after, Dr. James J. Walsh, class of 1884, who went on to become dean of the Fordham Medical School and one of the first editors of the *Catholic Encyclopedia* stated, "The disturbance of incomes and of feelings created by the Civil War led to a considerable drop in numbers, and this drop, instead of being made up after the war, continued for nearly a decade, until I believe the attendance once dropped to scarcely more than 125 (sic). As I

50

look back I wonder where did we get our fine baseball teams in those years?" (The actual lowest number was 166.)

Former St. John's President Father Augustus Thébaud, explained the low enrollment in terms of the fact that other liberal arts colleges were also small at the time and that, as Father Gannon later noted, "millionaires were still a novelty," especially Catholic ones. Father Thébaud wrote:

"In this country very few persons understand the immense difference between a university and a college. The gentlemen who compose the legislatures of the various states are so completely ignorant on this point that often when they grant a charter to a new college they give to the institutions the power of granting all the degrees granted by the highest and most complete universities in Europe.

"In the long but deceptive list of institutions in which the highest education is supposed to be given there are only two which, in general opinion, are real universities, Harvard and Yale. Are they universities in the sense that is attached to the word in Europe? They catalogue in their registers faculties of Letters, of Laws, of Medicine, of Divinity. But the same is true of many of the 72 universities to which that title has been granted by charter. Everyone admits that for the great majority of them it is a mere pretense.

"Harvard and Yale themselves do not require for admission into their freshman class anything like the requirements of European universities. When a young man presents himself to the Board of Examiners at Cambridge or Yale, he need have only pursued a course in any respectable academy or grammar school, and come prepared for the usual studies carried on in all the colleges of the Union.

"This is a tacit admission that their rule is not different from that of other colleges. The advantages the students expect to find there are a more aristocratic class of companions, a larger library, perhaps more experienced teachers in the ordinary

51

branches and undoubtedly more flashy lecturers on what is called 'modern science,' a very problematic way of understanding education.

"Columbia seems to me to have a great advantage over Princeton from the fact that there has always been connected with it a grammar school in which the pupils are prepared for college, while at Princeton the pupils are received from every quarter and the college course must feel the confusion resulting from so many differing feeders."

In fact, among the 21 Jesuit institutions in the U.S. and Canada at the time, there were only 1524 students en total and Fordham ranked 15th in the number of enrollees among them. Though there were problems at Fordham, the number of students was commensurate with its institutional peers.

Notable growth came to Fordham with the ascendancy of Irish-born Rev. Patrick F. Dealy as 12th president, when Father Gockeln was sent to Holy Cross College in Worcester, Massachusetts, in 1882.

Dealy's administration was said to be the beginning of a new era marked by the end of the conservative ways of the old French-trained Jesuits, and the dawn of control by younger men who were raised in the United States, though it was really just the beginning of an evolution that would continue over the next 125 years. The older set was resolute that the colleges and seminaries they controlled should be far away from city centers to keep "worldly temptation" away from students. (Though Fordham was relatively close to New York City, at its founding the train ride from Manhattan still took an hour and half.)

A former St. John's student from the first graduating class of the early 1840's, Father Dealy set out to change the culture on campus – and to bring New York City closer. He had seen the world, having studied in Belgium, Austria and Rome. As a teacher at St. Francis Xavier in Manhattan, he became well acquainted with the church hierarchy and local politicians. He even led the first American pilgrimage to the Vatican.

Father Robert Gannon wrote, "Too seldom in its history has Fordham been fortunate enough to find a leader who understood the domesticities and was at the same time familiar with the world outside the gate."

Catholicism in New York City was also growing. The Know-Nothings had been defeated and some, though certainly not all, prejudice had abated. Dealy took advantage of the new climate and fostered a connection between the city and the college. He was noted as "the most prominent Jesuit of his time in New York" and was credited with getting Mayor William R. Grace elected as the city's first Roman Catholic mayor. Grace was, of course, the great shipping magnate (W.R. Grace), a major philanthropist who co-founded the Grace Institute, dedicated to providing tuition-free education and training in business and administrative skills to economically disadvantaged women. (Grace ended up being a significant donor to Fordham was well.)

In his book, *Loyola and Montreal* (1962), Timothy P. Slattery wrote of Dealy, "…a new era began at Fordham. The conservative views of the older Jesuits gave way to his broader and more modern ideas, laying the basis of a free and constant contact with the life of the great city of New York."

With his comparatively more worldly and political thinking, one of Father Dealy's first acts was to allow publication of a newspaper, the *Fordham College Monthly*, later to be named the *Fordham Monthly* and then simply, *The Monthly*. It was first issued in November of 1882.

One of the first editors, hand chosen by the administration, wrote about being called to the Administration Building a month earlier: "It was a holiday for some reason or other; and about ten o'clock those who were to form the first board of editors were summoned to the vice-president's office…The meeting was called to order and the plot unfolded by Father Halpin, somewhat after this fashion: 'Boys we must have a paper. Every college of any consequence has one. A paper has never succeeded here. We must make a new trial. You are the board of editors. It is now in order to elect officers.'"

In 1883 Fordham football was born. The first game was played on November 26th against St. Francis Xavier. Edward's Parade, not yet named, was the first official football field. After a slow start, the college actually decided to abandon baseball to concentrate its efforts on the gridiron. Though Fordham continued the horrible losing streak that began at the program's inception, the scores began to get closer over time. The "Maroons" were born (teams were not yet called The Rams) and the foundation was laid for a football program that would be acclaimed a few decades later. Eventually, baseball would return.

Dealy also set out to beautify the campus by paving the roads and upgrading the lawns and general appearance of the school. He had frescoes painted in the University Church and saw that it was improved greatly.

As a number of buildings had also fallen into decay, he fixed those as well, and made improvements to drainage. Dealy instituted lessons in horsemanship, dancing, boxing and fencing. There were plans for a swimming pool that did not materialize.

To Fordham students who have long been told of tunnels that run beneath the various buildings, here is the proof. Father Dealy oversaw the construction of underground pathways through which pipes for boilers to replace the fireplaces would pass from building to building. Reports that these tunnels – and a number of buildings on campus – are haunted remain only legend.

In April 1879, Pelham Avenue (now Fordham Road) was constructed. Rumor had it that the city was going to take the property east of Southern Boulevard, which it did in 1885 by order of condemnation for $93,966.25, a ridiculously low amount. This was beautiful property where students had long enjoyed the woods and the river. From that point on, students would be mere visitors as the land was turned into the New York Botanical Gardens and the Bronx Zoo.

The loss of property also meant moving the Jesuit graveyard that had existed on the eastern part of the property, now no longer a part of their domain. It is reported that between January 21st and 28th of 1890, during the dead of winter, the remains of 61 Jesuits, three seminarians, nine college students and two workmen, were somehow transferred to the new cemetery plot that stands in the shadow of the University Church. The remains of one brother and one workman were not found. The transfers were meticulously documented in Latin and English by Fr. Joseph Zwinge, S.J., a college administrator. Among those in repose were Fathers Thébaud, Legouais, Doucet and Tissot. Jesuits are now buried at the Auriesville Jesuit Cemetery in Montgomery County, New York, but until 1909 the plot with those reinterred bodies was used for the departed priests at Fordham.

Though realized after Father Dealy's administration, he is given credit for laying the groundwork for introduction of military instruction among students. With consent from Washington, he took advantage of a recent act of Congress that provided that U.S. Army officers be detailed at certain schools and colleges throughout the country to instruct students in military science and tactics.

From 1885 to 1890, a veteran of the 7th U.S. Cavalry in the Dakotas, Lt. Herbert C. Squiers, eventually built a cadet battalion to a strength of 200. It was a precursor to the modern ROTC (Reserve Officers' Training Corps). The first corps consisted of a dozen students, but rose to almost 50 by the end of the first year. They had fatigues and full dress uniforms of gray with brass buttons and gold lace. They wore black helmets similar to those worn by the cadets at West Point and carried rifles.

The cadets were a major presence at the 1887 commencement exercises, where they put on an exhibition drill, the start of a tradition that lasted at least until 1905. They were also considered partly responsible for an increase in student enrollment, which was again getting close to 300.

When Lt. Squiers left Fordham to fight the Sioux Indians during the Indian Wars in 1890, he was succeeded by a man whose surname, at least, is known to almost everyone who visits the Fordham campus. Edward's Parade (Eddie's to today's students), one of every undergraduate's favorite spots at Rose Hill, was named for Clarence Ransom Edwards, then a second lieutenant in the First United States Infantry and a fresh-faced recent graduate of the U.S. Military Academy at West Point.

Clarence R. Edwards of Edwards Parade fame.

Taller than six feet and an Ohio native, Edwards was a commanding presence who became a revered role model. He was strict and ordered the cadets to act like gentlemen, even to salute faculty members as they passed. Not a Catholic, he was somehow able to mix military exercises with prayer by ordering a musket salute during candlelight services. The corps would salute the Virgin Mary by firing their muskets four times.

Edwards went on to serve in the Philippines and eventually became a famous World War I hero who headed the "Yankee" or 26th U.S. Army Division of New England and became a Brigadier General. He died in 1931 and was buried in Arlington National Cemetery.

The college opened Science Hall in 1886, now known as Freeman Hall. Another project conceived of and begun by

Father Dealy, but finished during Father Campbell's reign, the structure offered more legitimacy to science in the curriculum, a change brought on partly by the Industrial Revolution. It took a while, however, for the labs to be fitted with equipment. In addition, a three-year Bachelor of Science degree was created under the direction of Father Freeman, the science professor. The first degree was conferred in 1875. Taken away and then reinstituted, the science curriculum was considered to be something of a commercial program and not respected like its liberal arts counterpart.

It would be some time before studying science was considered on par with studying the humanities, in fact. There was a great deal of debate during this period about whether the Jesuits should branch out into the sciences. Many thought they should have confined their institutions of higher education to their specialty – operating small liberal arts colleges. Science was considered a "trade," like plumbing. Practical education of any kind was beneath many of those in the Society of Jesus at the

Photo: Fordham Archives

The Gabelli School of Business, long known as Hughes Hall, and the first home of Fordham Prep.

time. Father Thomas Gannon, president from 1891 to 1896, repudiated the existence of a "commercial" track in a letter to the editor of the Jesuit publication, *The Woodstock Letters*. He said, "Now there exists no longer such a course and I consider it a subject for great congratulation to St. John's that it has at length rid itself of this demoralizing course which was generally rated as the 'Refuge of Idlers.'"

Father Robert Gannon wrote about this era years later: "It is even suggested that preoccupation with professional, semi-professional, and even vocational schools, above all preoccupation with sheer numbers, has been responsible for cheapening the arts course itself to the point where an A.B. (B.A.) is now conferred on candidates who never learned a word of Classical Latin, let alone Greek! They tell of a recent bachelor of arts who was asked the meaning of *E pluribus unum* (Out of many, one) and answered 'In God We Trust.'"

Again, the number of students was growing with the influx of Catholic immigrants to the U.S. Archbishop Hughes' dreams of prestige and power for Catholics was being realized as the church's numbers grew steadily in the years following the war. Catholics, particularly those of Irish descent, were becoming a more powerful force in New York City politics.

Like those of his predecessors, Campbell's first presidential tenure was very short, but he would return a few years later. During the last year of his first term, 1888, he made his mark by installing the first electric lights at the Rose Hill campus. The first incandescent bulbs were placed in the cellar of Science Hall, in the first and second division study halls, and in the student dining rooms. Electricity would cost $1800 per

Photo: Fordham Archives

The Statue of Archbishop John Hughes as it appeared early on. The inscription is written in Latin.

year at first, and the lights would be turned off at 9 p.m. After that, everyone had to use oil lamps.

Only 37 years old when he became president, Father Campbell made an impression that led him to bigger and better things. As he left Fordham to become Provisional of the New York-Maryland province of the Society of Jesus, he was replaced by Rev. John Scully, born in Brooklyn and raised in Sandy Hill, New York. Father Scully had studied in Canada and England and had been a professor at Georgetown and St. Peter's College in Jersey City.

Scully embarked on a construction plan of his own, but he had to hurry because he'd be out by mid-1891. He built a new Junior Hall for the Second Division (high school) students that cost $75,000. It was called Hughes Hall after the college founder and opened in 1890 with a gym, billiards room, classrooms, dormitory and more. Until 1972 it housed Fordham Prep. He also proceeded to extend what was then known as Senior Hall, adding the west wing of today's Dealy.

The golden jubilee of St. John's College arrived in 1891. A huge celebration was scheduled precisely 50 years after the original dedication, June 24, 1891. Father Scully, still president at the time, presided alongside Father Patrick Dealy, the former president.

The long-awaited unveiling of a statue to honor Archbishop Hughes would mark the day. The sculpture remains standing today behind the Administration Building. William Rudolf O'Donovan, a well-known sculptor of the time, produced the bronze caste. Having cost $10,000, the statue depicts Archbishop Hughes in his Episcopal robes with a book in his hands, as if he is delivering an address. It is eight feet, two inches high and is mounted on a granite pedestal. The site was restored in 1941 by that year's graduating class.

Unfortunately, the commencement ceremony that was part of the jubilee graduated only nine bachelors students, far fewer than the 13 who graduated in 1866, 25 years earlier. There were 351 students school-wide.

The New York Times story from the next day had the following headline: "St. John's Half Century: An interesting anniversary at the Fordham College." The newspaper wrote:

"The beautiful grounds of St. John's College at Fordham never presented a more exhilarating and picturesque scene than they did yesterday, when was celebrated the golden jubilee of the foundation of the institution in 1841, and the forty-sixth Commencement of the college, these events being signalized by the unveiling of a fine statue of the late Archbishop John Hughes.

"The American flag was everywhere. The long, winding, elm-shaded driveway was brilliant in red, white and blue, while the national colors floated from the college buildings and the immense canvas pavilion beneath which the jubilee services were held. Fully 5,000 people participated in the latter, the throng including many distinguished prelates, notable among whom were Archbishop Ryan of Philadelphia, Bishop Loughlin of Brooklyn, Bishop O'Farrell of Trenton, N.J., and nearly every priest of prominence in the Sees of New York and Long Island.

"The exercises began at 10 o'clock with the celebration of a pontifical militans (sic) high mass, in which Archbishop Corrigan was the celebrant, the Rev. John Scully, S.J., deacon; the Rev. P.F. Dealy, S.J., sub deacon."

The Times further reported that there was a battalion drill of the Corps of Cadets under the command of Lieutenant Edwards, the unveiling of the Hughes statue, a salutatory address by James A. Dunn of the graduating class and the reading of a jubilee poem entitled "50 Years" by Dr. James M. Butler.

Judge Morgan O'Brien, the previously noted alumnus who was president of the alumni association, said, "the history of St. John's College was like a beautiful dream, the scenes of which had unfolded through 50 years culminated in the magnificent demonstration and significant votive offering. The history of the Fordham College was an epitome of the life of John Hughes."

As the statue was revealed with the pulling of a cord holding American flags, the newspaper said, "the great crowd shouted itself hoarse, the band played and guns were fired by the field battery."

Archbishop Ryan, chosen to give the keynote address, said, "Today the great statue of a man is unveiled, and under circumstances and with environments which give additional luster to the occasion. On this day 50 years ago the illustrious prelate, John Hughes, then Bishop of New York, opened this institution of learning as a seminary for the education of young priests of his diocese. It was one of the great acts of his episcopate. And now, after a half century, the devoted sons of Ignatius desire to celebrate the golden jubilee of this institution by having unveiled the first public statue of a man who, like themselves, was ever found in the vanguard of the army who fought the battle for the true and the good...He had confidence that the great American mind would yet understand the value of religious education, and acknowledge that the Old Church was right in her position that it was essential to the well-being of society."

Shortly after the jubilee, Fr. Thomas Gannon, S.J., who would remain for five years, replaced Father Scully. It was during the late 1800's that the St. John's College Alumni Association was founded. In 1893, the group held a banquet at the Hotel Savoy attended by Diamond Jim Brady, the famous mayor of New York City, and Lillian Russell, the famous stage actress and singer, who were an item.

The *Fordham Monthly* of March 1893 wrote:

"Served on Dresden china, in a dining-room of royal dimensions, to the accompaniment of sweet strains of music, for the gratification and exhilaration of the flower of Alma Mater's sons, the Fordham Alumni Banquet of 1893 may well be

61

recorded as the most memorable in the history of the Alumni Association. The banquet was in every sense a happy and consoling event." *The Monthly* reported that nine courses were served with five wines. Judge O'Brien and another alumnus, Charles C. Marrin, gave speeches.

An early graduate, Edward Murphy, Jr., class of 1857, was lauded that night. Murphy had become a member of the U.S. Senate from New York that year. Having been Chairman of the Democratic State Committee, he was one of the most powerful politicians in the state and was credited with helping former New York State Governor Grover Cleveland get the six votes he needed to become a candidate for the presidency, though Murphy is reported to have broken with Cleveland later on.

The New York Times wrote in Murphy's 1911 obituary that he "earned the displeasure of President Cleveland by forcing into the Wilson Tariff bill a high protective tariff on collars, cuffs, shirts and other garments produced by Troy factories (his home turf) and by concurring in other high tariff duties on manufactured articles in return for support in behalf of these duties." Murphy had been part of the political circle of Samuel Tilden, the former New York State Governor who had run for president unsuccessfully in 1876.

The following year, General Martin T. McMahon, the class of 1855's Civil War hero, spoke at the alumni event held at the legendary Delmonico's restaurant in Manhattan.

As the Spanish-American War was beginning, the college saluted a number of alumni who had volunteered, among them Robert Foresque from Fordham Prep who was one of Teddy Roosevelt's Rough Riders. Dr. George McCreery, class of 1874, an army surgeon, died after contracting a fever.

Fordham ended the 19th century on a down note. Enrollment had again shrunk to just over 500 and the old manor house, the original building on the Manor Fordham (1692) that was home to the Watts family and thought to have been a refuge for General

Washington, was torn down under the direction of Father Thomas Campbell, an 1896 move derided by many. For many years it had been used as the college infirmary. Campbell, called "unsentimental," had returned to the presidency to succeed Father Gannon. Two years later, in 1898, Fordham was officially made part of the Borough of the Bronx when the area that was once the Manor Fordham, one of several Westchester County towns, was consolidated into one of New York City's five boroughs. The area around Rose Hill would have better days and worse days. The same was the case for the soon-to-be full-fledged university whose fiscal health was a continuing issue.

Chapter IV:
Fordham Embarks on the Twentieth Century

By the year 1901, the U.S. at large was in a good place. Teddy Roosevelt was president and there was peace and a good deal of prosperity. Henry Ford's automobile was taking hold and the U.S. was moving towards a manufacturing and industrial economy. The titans of industry were providing jobs for the masses.

At Fordham, there was yet another new president, Father George A. Pettit, 42.

The Bronx had changed quite a bit. Southern Boulevard cut off the vast land to the east that once made Fordham part of a much larger parcel.

The Third Avenue El was extended from Tremont Avenue to Fordham's gate by 1911, which cost a few more acres of land. The result was that proportionally more students became commuters, a trend that would continue through most of the 20th century.

Discipline and order had become an issue by this time. There were reports that students were even visiting prostitutes. We know they were smoking because the college actually started selling cigarettes to the young men in 1892. Other offenses were leaving the campus without permission, staying out all night, drinking and fighting. Expulsion was a typical consequence. By this time, flogging had been (mostly) made a thing of the past.

A number of well-known students had entered the college, including George Carnegie, the nephew of industrialist and steel magnate Andrew Carnegie, and James O'Neill, brother of playwright Eugene O'Neill and son of the famous actor, also named James (model for the James Tyrone character in *Long Day's Journey Into Night*). While the young Carnegie had a rather nefarious reputation, young James O'Neill (Jamie) was well regarded as a poet who contributed to *The Monthly*. Unfortunately, Jamie was eventually expelled, supposedly for bringing a prostitute to campus, part of a prank detailed in his brother's play, *A Moon for the Misbegotten* (1947). As the story goes, Jamie introduced the woman to the Jesuits as his sister. But, when she used an expletive in a priest's presence, the jig was up. It was also said that this story could not have been true because the Fordham Jesuits would have known that James O'Neill did not have a sister. Jamie was permitted to leave Fordham with the credits he had earned, though he did not continue his college education.

The extension of the train line was also responsible for a significant growth in the area's population and farmland was giving way to houses and even apartment buildings. The Grand Concourse, modeled on the Champs-Élysées in Paris, was built between 1894 and 1909. Designed by Louis Aloys Risse, an Alsatian immigrant who had previously worked for the New York Central Railroad and later appointed chief topographical engineer for the city, it had eleven lanes for traffic and a tree-lined divider. It would take people from 138th Street to Mosholu Parkway, just north of Fordham. Initially, at least, the Concourse brought New Yorkers who could afford ornate, classic style buildings. By 1900, the population of the Bronx had reached more than 200,000 people and Fordham's campus was now an oasis amid the bustle of the city.

The college was not growing quickly enough for its leaders. It was still trailing its contemporaries, especially with regard to fundraising. There was a huge mortgage at the time; reports put it in the hundreds of thousands of dollars, though the exact figure is disputed.

Proceeds from the sale of property did lead to more construction, most notably College Hall (the future Collins Auditorium), a red brick building with a Roman portico on the site of the old Rose Hill Manor House that was called "jarring" at the time. But, even back then there were delays due to union

Collins Auditorium, seen here, was named after Bishop John Collins, president in the early 1900's.

issues and cost overruns. A bricklayers' strike put work on hold, as did the installation of still another college president, Father (later Bishop) John Collins, 47, a Kentucky-born former missionary. Finally, College Hall was dedicated in 1905 with theatre space for productions, classrooms and locker space in the basement for the growing number of day students. More land was soon sold, this time a four-acre plot bordering Southern Boulevard. It would house Fordham Hospital to be operated by the city, also the future clinical home of the soon-to-be established Fordham Medical School.

In 1902, basketball debuted at Fordham. The first game was played against Brooklyn Polytechnic Institute; the Rams lost 18-10. It took time for the basketball team to take root, but football was now thriving. Under team captain Ed Glennon, a future New York State Supreme Court Justice, the team beat NYU, Rensselaer Polytechnic Institute and Delaware; it also tied with Villanova. Shortly after that season, the NCAA was born to rule over college athletics.

Track was also introduced as a sport with the Track Association's first meet held in 1904. The *New York Herald* reported that Yale, Princeton and Columbia competed that day and that two Fordham men took first place in their competitions. A Mr. Fallon won the 60-yard dash while a Mr. Duffy led the 60-

yard invitational. (Newspapers did not always report first names in those days.)

The St. John's curriculum by then consisted of a junior division (the preparatory school), requiring four years of study in Latin, Greek, grammar, literature, history, geography, mathematics and religion; and a senior division (the college), requiring three years of study in "poetry" (humanities), rhetoric and philosophy. An Artium Baccalaureus (Bachelor of Arts) was earned for completion of both curricula, and an additional year of philosophy would earn a Magister Artium (Masters of Arts). There was also a "commercial" track similar to that of a modern business school, offered as an alternative to the classical curriculum, which awarded a certificate instead of a degree upon completion.

These changes were mandated by the State of New York, which decreed in 1895 that a college would be defined as a four-year school requiring four years of secondary education for admission. The Jesuit schools previously had a seven-year track that sometimes hampered graduating students from admission to law and medical schools. With the directive that standards set by the state Board of Regents be applied to denominational and other secondary schools, there was no choice but to adopt the state system. Both Columbia and New York University were emerging at that time as leaders of higher education for those who were not Catholic. Fordham was thus taking its place for those that were.

Little old St. John's College began to expand by more than a building at a time. On June 21, 1904, with the authorization of the regents of the University of the State of New York, the board of trustees gave the go-ahead for a School of Law and a School of Medicine. At the 1905 commencement, Father Collins made the grand announcement that the Fordham Law School and Medical School would become a reality. With these additions, St. John's College was to be renamed Fordham University (St. John's

University already existed). The change was made official in 1907, though the collegiate department would retain its name until the charter was changed to make it Fordham College in 1931. It was also made official that the high school and college would exist as separate entities and the medical school would become affiliated with Fordham Hospital.

That same year the Fordham Fight Song debuted. John Ignatius Coveney, its author and a Fordham student, first presented the piece at the Carnegie Lyceum on May 1 during a performance by the Fordham University Drama and Glee Club:

Hail! Men of Fordham, hail! On to the fray!
Once more our foes assail in strong
array.
Once more the old Maroon, waves
on high
We'll sing our battle song.
We do or die.

With a Ram, a Ram, a Ram for
victory
With a Ram, a Ram, a Ram for
loyalty.
To the fight, to fight,
To win our laurels bright!

Hail! Men of Fordham, hail! On to the fray!
Once more our foes assail in strong array.
Once more the old Maroon, waves on high
We'll sing our battle song.
We do or die.

Coveney was a football player and member of the debate team who also wrote poetry for *The Monthly*. He is credited with

68

writing the fight song for the Boston Red Sox and, per legend, was ghostwriter of the classic, "By the Light of the Silvery Moon." Coveney died very early in life in 1911, his death attributed to overwork, fever and lack of sleep.

While Father Collins was popular and did a great deal to further the growth of the university, he was nonetheless replaced after only two years, having been sent by Pope Pius X to become Administrator Apostolic of Jamaica, the West Indies, where he had previously served as a missionary. Next up to the presidency (number 19) was Rev. Daniel J. Quinn, a 42-year-old Jesuit who had no administrative experience, though he did have the advantage of being a native New Yorker.

It should be stated here that the short terms of Fordham presidents until this time and into the 1930's were the result of a Jesuit rule that university presidents serve three-year terms capped at two terms each. It was a tradition that probably led to some of the university's failures since no president was able to serve long enough to make lasting change.

Father Quinn inherited the financial troubles of his predecessor and was given the job of trying to get Fordham out of debt, a job at which he did not succeed.

Aside from the fact that the medical school was costing money, he also gave the teachers a raise to $400 per year if they lived on campus and $600 if they had families and lived on their own. If they ate a hot meal at Fordham, $50 per year was deducted annually.

Fordham Law School was an almost immediate success. With 13 initial students, there were 230 by 1911. Enrollment increased to 687 by 1920 and 1,484 by 1925. The nomadic law school was first placed at Rose Hill in Collins Auditorium. It soon moved to Manhattan, with stops at 42 Broadway, 20 Vesey Street, 140 Nassau Street, the Woolworth Building and finally, 302 Broadway, where it stayed until the Lincoln Center Campus was built in the 1960's.

Even though admission to the New York State Bar required only two years of study in law school, the Fordham School of Law was established with a three-year curriculum ending in an LL.D. The strength of the law school was attributed to an attorney named Paul Fuller, the first dean. He later went on to become President Woodrow Wilson's personal envoy to Mexico. Fuller knew how to structure the school and hired the right professors, including some of New York City's most prominent lawyers. He and Professor Ralph W. Gifford were reportedly the first to introduce the "case method" to study law. Unlike the medical school, it was said to have been easier to start a law school because it was a lot cheaper. Less equipment and space were needed and large lectures could be held instead of more individualized instruction.

Among the early graduates of Fordham Law School, two became Chief Justice of the New York State Court of Appeals, John T. Loughran and Albert Conway. In 1913, 88% of the Fordham men who took the New York State Bar Exam passed. At the time there was an 11% passing rate, so Fordham was doing something right.

The Fordham University Press, begun in 1908, came into its own a few years later and was churning out textbooks by Fordham professors. According to its web page in 2013, the publisher was established "not only to represent and uphold the values and traditions of the University itself, but also to further those values and traditions through the dissemination of scholarly research and ideas." The first book was *The Makers of Modern Medicine* by Dr. James J. Walsh, dean of the medical school. The Fordham University Press has published 2,500 books and maintains 1,000 active titles, including print and electronic. It is now housed in Canisius Hall, just outside the southeast Rose Hill entrance, next to Faculty Memorial Hall.

In 1910, the Seismic Observatory, today modernized and located just east of Freeman Hall, was installed in the basement

70

of the Administration Building. Now named for William Spain, a student from the class of 1925 who died unexpectedly, its update in the 1920's was a gift from his family. The first seismic recordings from this location are the oldest in the region and among the oldest in the U.S. Even in 1924, the station was able to detect an earthquake that occurred on April 23rd in Corinth, Greece, the site of an 1858 earthquake that destroyed that entire city. A plaque of St. Emidio, patron saint of earthquakes, hangs on the door of the observatory building. A working model of the Fordham Seismic Station was the only individual university exhibit at the 1939 World's Fair. In 1924, the observatory was formally dedicated and moved to the site of today's Loyola Hall. It was relocated to Keating in 1927 and to its present spot in 1931.

Father Quinn's tenure as president lasted until 1911 when Rev. Thomas J. McCluskey replaced him. At age 54, he lasted just

Photo: Fordham Archives
The College of Pharmacy Building, now Thébaud Hall.

four years in the job and inherited a debt of $600,000.

Expansion continued in 1912 when the College of Pharmacy was added. It offered a three-year program in pharmacy. Ecumenical for its

day, the College of Pharmacy had a mainly Jewish student body. Owing to that fact, pharmacy students were exempt from the then-required course in Catholic theology. The school's longtime dean, Jacob Diner, was also Jewish. Pharmacy did not become a Bachelor's program until the late 1930's. A school of dentistry was proposed, but never came to fruition.

71

By 1912, the university had a total of 548 students under 124 professors. There were 255 law students with 12 professors, 164 medical students with 96 professors and 160 students in what was known as the "academical" department under 16 professors. By 1914, there were 1,700 students, 400 in the law school.

The College of St. Francis Xavier, Fordham's Manhattan branch, founded in 1861, was closed in 1913 and united with the uptown school. Various additional colleges were soon established. In 1916, Fordham opened its Teachers College in the Woolworth Building, the tallest building in Manhattan at the time, at 51 stories and 750 feet, and arguably, the city's most prestigious address. Now known as the Graduate School of Education, the school was encouraged by yet another cardinal produced by Fordham, John Cardinal Farley, class of 1867. Farley, the Archbishop of New York, was on a mission to increase the number of Catholics in the teaching profession and to establish a Catholic professional class in New York City.

The education school allowed women to study at Fordham decades before the establishment of the all-women Thomas More College in 1964. Though, it could be argued that the teachers' college back then was more of a training program for teachers than a college. Also added were the School of Sociology and Social Service and the Graduate School of Fordham University, later the Graduate School of Arts and Sciences, which then offered Masters degrees in philosophy, English literature and pedagogy (education).

The story of the Fordham University Medical School does not end well. Having lasted from September 28, 1905 until 1921, it was apparently never given the financial support it needed – mostly because the university didn't have the funds at the time and because those in charge did not realize what kind of investment was needed. They did not immediately install laboratories and equipment; they didn't even dedicate enough space. Only a portion of the science building was given to the medical school at its inception, though by 1913 it had its own building later named Old Chemistry (now the dorm, Finlay Hall) near Bathgate Avenue. Reputedly, it was located there to get the corpses in and out efficiently, which began years of speculation, even today, that the building is haunted.

The first dean, who only lasted the first school year, was not the right choice and didn't hire sufficiently committed and credentialed instructors, many of whom were only part-time employees. Even though there was an affiliation with Fordham Hospital, the university didn't have its own hospital. This led to a relatively low rating by the Flexner Report commissioned by the Carnegie Foundation to grade medical schools at the time.

Nonetheless, there were some high points. The student body was considered respectable; many had been recruited from schools like Holy Cross, St. Francis Xavier

Is Finlay Hall, Once Home to Fordham Medical School, Haunted?

Finlay Hall, before becoming a dorm, was Fordham's Medical School, built at a cost of $148,937.58 in 1912. In the lofted rooms students could observe dissections of cadavers and the basement served as the holding place for bodies.

More than once, students have woken up in the middle of the night, feeling as though someone is grabbing at their throat making it difficult for them to breathe or feel a tugging on their toe as if they were a cadaver being tagged.

They also sometimes see what looks like students peering down on them from the loft.

Photo: Fordham Archives

and Fordham, itself. Under Dean James Walsh, an author and entrepreneur who had earlier been invited to speak at the White House by President Theodore Roosevelt, the school made some strides. A doctor and well-regarded expert of his time on diseases of the nervous system, Walsh earned a national reputation on the topic. He made neuroscience a specialty at Fordham Medical School and was also able to procure a "Class A" ranking by the American Medical Association in 1914.

Dr. Walsh, an 1884 St. John's College graduate, was famous at Rose Hill for sending his students out of the classroom and into the neighboring New York Zoological Society and Botanical Garden to perform field research. He was also well respected for having studied in Paris, Vienna and Berlin after he earned his doctorate from the University of Pennsylvania.

The New York Sun reported on September 17, 1912:

"The medical department of Fordham University has inaugurated an extension course on affections of the mind and nervous system which is highly creditable to that institution. Eminent specialists from London, Zurich, Madrid, Montreal, Albany and Washington are delivering a course of lectures on diagnosis, physiology, pathology, surgery and other management of diseases of the nervous system, to which the attention of the medical profession has been called...and which deserve to be patronized by all physicians who aim to keep abreast of progress in medicine.

"In recognition of their valuable services to science and humanity and to the university, the president of the latter has conferred various degrees on the eminent lecturers, and by banquet and other well-earned compliments the faculty has made the occasion memorable in the annals of medical education in this country."

Dr. Carl Jung of the University of Zurich and a famous psychologist who was about to break with the teaching of

Sigmund Freud, was a visiting professor, which drew a great deal of attention from the newspapers and the medical community.

Dean Walsh, unfortunately, resigned when he realized he did not have the support of Father McCloskey.

Ultimately, the medical school failed because it wasn't able to attract enough students, was never able to raise enough money to operate properly and, perhaps, because it didn't have the right leadership. Some attributed the lack of funds to World War 1 and the resulting poor state of the U.S. economy. Others believed it was a lack of commitment on the part of the university.

Many presidents have spoken of reopening the medical school. As recently as 2009, Fordham began negotiations with New York Medical College regarding the possible merger of the two institutions. That did not happen, but the schools maintain a close academic relationship and provide joint courses. The relationship is expected to grow in the coming years.

NYS Governor Martin H. Glynn, Fordham Class of 1894, formally nominated Woodrow Wilson for president.

The Rev. Joseph Mulry had been appointed president of Fordham in 1915. A New Yorker and alum, he entered the Jesuits at the age of 15. Mulry had four brothers, three of whom were priests. The fourth, Thomas M. Mulry, was a well-known philanthropist and president of Emigrant Industrial Savings Bank, founded by the Mulry family. Father Mulry had also been president of St. Peter's College and of the alumni organization, which had been dormant for a number of years. It was officially re-launched in 1915 as the

Fordham College Alumni Association and incorporated as an independent entity. At that year's banquet and reunion, Mulry, told the group, "You belong to Fordham and Fordham belongs to you." He encouraged the beginnings of alumni associations in other states and cities, one as far away as Denver.

Just as the new president took office, it was time for another jubilee. The 75th anniversary of Fordham was held on June 14th to coincide with commencement and marked the first time all the schools held their ceremonies together. It was the first commencement held outdoors since Collins Auditorium had been built. There were 8,000 guests.

With World War I raging in Europe, Father Mulry said that day, "The thrones of kings are tottering while the dread roll of battle drums echoes 'round the world.'" It just so happened that President Wilson was re-nominated for a second term that very day, his popularity bolstered by the belief that he was keeping the U.S. out of the war.

Almost simultaneously, the president's nomination speech was being delivered at the Democratic National Convention in St. Louis by a Fordham graduate, the Hon. Martin H. Glynn, class of 1894, who had been New York's 40th governor (1913-14) and the first Catholic to hold that post. Former President Theodore Roosevelt called the speech the chief factor in President Wilson's re-election. Glynn, placed in office because his predecessor was impeached, was a longtime politician who had also been owner and publisher of the *Albany Times Union*. He was perhaps most famous for a 1919 article, "The Crucifixion of the Jews Must Stop!" in *The American Hebrew*, where he lamented the poor conditions of European Jews after World War I and referred to their condition as a potential "holocaust." He went on to assert, "six million Jewish men and women are starving across the seas." Sadly, Glynn committed suicide in 1924 at the age of 53 after having suffered from chronic back pain from a spinal injury. The former governor had remained close to Fordham. He gave the commencement address in 1913 when he was lieutenant governor.

At the jubilee/commencement, 33 honorary degrees were given and *The Maroon*, the student yearbook debuted. Among the honorary degree recipients was Augustin M. O'Neil of Staten Island, the oldest alumnus who, at 92, was among the college's first graduates in the class of 1849. O'Neil had been a second lieutenant in the Union Army's 69th Regiment during the Civil War and was noted for bravery at the Battle of Gettysburg.

Another dignitary in attendance was Fordham's own John Cardinal Farley, the Archbishop. Little did Cardinal Farley know that day he was handing a Fordham diploma to another man who would later be Archbishop of New York, a young Francis Joseph Spellman who would go on to fame and glory as a world-renowned prelate/politician. (More about Spellman later.)

At the jubilee ceremony, Cardinal Farley said, "As I sat listening to the discourses today, my mind ran back to when I was a student on these grounds. I recalled the stories of two young students [the McMahon brothers who died in the Civil War], fired by that love of patriotism, who stepped down from the steps of the old mansion, marched down the lawn to the city and into the ranks of the army going to the front." He also noted that Father Patrick Dealy had been his favorite teacher.

In the *Woodstock Letters*, a Jesuit monthly, Rev. Edward I Devitt, S.J., reported:

"On the athletic field just back of First Division, with the tall elms for a background, a magnificent symbolic forum had been erected. In the central semi-circular portico, surmounted by a dome, was a dais for the presiding dignitaries. Just behind them were places for the deans of the schools of Arts, Medicine, and Law, and around this central dais sat the faculties of the university, those who were to receive honorary degrees and invited guests. The number of columns supporting this semi-circular portico was 20, coincident with the number of presidents

77

of the university since its foundation. To the right and left of this central portico were two others backed by seventy-five columns arranged in double rows to signify the 75th anniversary of the university. The right side was reserved for the graduates, the left for the alumni. In colors on the lower inside shell of the dome was the university seal, and on the top of the dome a central cross."

At the time of the anniversary, the U.S. was still one year away from entering the war, but it was becoming clear that Wilson's isolationist stance would be broken and that U.S. troops would be deployed. Fordham had discontinued its military drill corps by this time, but it was soon reintroduced. Fordham's young men were gearing up.

The Monthly wrote the following, referring to General McMahon, the surviving McMahon brother, "War may come. We do not desire it, and fervently pray God that it may, with honor and in justice, be averted. But if it does come there are ten thousand other McMahons, among them the men of Fordham, to carry on the traditions which he so honorably upheld."

It wrote later, directing its words to President Wilson: "In this dark hour of trial the sons of Fordham, past and present, are enlisted in your support to the last man…Command us. We are absolutely yours, for we hear in your voice the command of the Almighty."

Major Robert W. Patterson of the U.S. Army Medical Corps approached Father Mulry, who was known to have been committed to the war effort, to suggest that the university form an ambulance corps to supplement the army's own. In short order, there were more than 100 student enrollees. The endeavor was partly funded by alumni and partly by the Red Cross.

Again there was a banquet at the Waldorf Astoria, a proper send-off to the members of what became known as the Fordham University Overseas Ambulance Corps. In attendance was the heralded Brigadier General Clarence Ransom Edwards (the previously noted cadet corps commander) who delivered a stirring address. There was a presentation of the colors – a silk American flag and a silk Maroon flag with the year 1917, and the group's name in silver letters.

Father Mulry told the recruits to "remember that they were going forth as Catholics who hear God's call in the call of your country and who see God's face in the folds of the flag.

The volunteers were sworn into the Army and shipped out on June 14, 1917, under Captain Joseph E. Donnelly, an instructor in Surgery and Laryngology at the Fordham Medical School. They sailed for France in August on the U.S.S. Baltic and were divided into three sections, S.S.U. 551, 552 and 553. During a year and a half of active service, unit 551 alone evacuated more than 40,000 soldiers of the French Army, many during the Champagne Offensive. Twenty-six members of the 552 received regimental or divisional citations. Unit 553 received two section citations and 29 of its members were awarded the French Croix de Guerre (War Cross).

As detailed in *The Maroon* (1920), Charles A. Curtin, born in 1897, was a student from Shenandoah, Pennsylvania. Later a lawyer who settled in Manhattan, *The Maroon* reported the following account of his service in the Fordham Ambulance Corps:

Members of the Fordham University Overseas Ambulance Corps, Section 553.

"The members…made their way to Le Havre and a three-day train ride to Saint-Nazaire in the legendary '40 and 8s,' box cars made to hold eight horses now crammed with forty men. There, the Fordham men were divided and were attached to three French units for action. But it was not until March 1918 that they experienced the full magnitude of the war.

"Curtin's French Division moved to support the English front at Ville Quemont, near Saint-Quentin. For ten days the Germans pushed the English and French back toward the Oise River. The wounded flooded the hospitals, and Curtin and his comrades worked days and nights without food or rest to move the

Charles A. Curtin and the Red Cross armband he wore in France. The stamp says, Ministere De La Guerre (War Ministry).

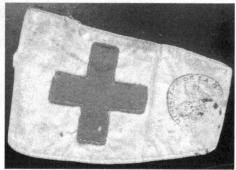

wounded to the rear as the Germans rushed onward. They stopped exhausted at Noyon.

"As Curtin's ambulance pushed on through the carnage, he pulled troops aboard with wounds gaping, bleeding. There were nine wounded in a Ford built for four; two were on the fenders and two on the floor with their feet on the running boards. The 'Tommy' next to him asked for a 'fag.' Curtin gave him a cigarette and asked about his wound. 'Oh, nothing much, only a ball,' he replied, opening his tunic to reveal a hole in his chest where the bullet had gone in and come out the back.

"Before they reached the hospital, the man was dead, Curtin recalled, 'with a cigarette in his fingers and a smile on his lips.'"

Curtin's humor hid his real feelings about his experiences in France. According to members of his family alive today, he was

80

so traumatized by events there that he refused to ever drive a car again and later on only related stories about the hijinks of his comrades, not the gory details of helping the war wounded.

The *Woodstock Letters* printed the following letter from a Y.M.C.A. official in France to Father Mulry:

Dear Sir:

Permit me to convey to you my high appreciation of the splendid work your institution is doing in sending out such a fine set of young men as those who compose the Ambulance section with which I have been associated for several weeks. I am myself a school man, professor of sociology and economics Southwestern University, Georgetown, Texas, and am now working under the auspices of the Y.M.C.A. among French soldiers. For three weeks I took my meals with the Fordham boys and daily witnessed them as they got their letters and boxes from home and I give you my testimony that nowhere in France have I found finer types of American manhood. They were strong, clean, wholesome fellows who are a credit to their school, their homes and their country. May God bless you in the good work you are doing.

Very truly yours, John C. Granbery

Many of those who did not join the ambulance corps, enlisted in the "Fighting Sixty-Ninth" New York regiment, which was previously a draw to those from Fordham.

By the time American troops arrived in France in June 1918, 1,520 Fordham alumni were in the armed services. (The Selective Service Act was passed by Congress in May of that year and signed by the president).

That summer, Congress also passed the "Students' Army Training Corps" (SATC) authorizing the establishment of units at American colleges and universities. In a telegram to Fr. Mulry, the Adjutant General of the Army wrote, "It is intended to discourage hasty and premature enlistment for active service on the part of young men, who though government by patriotic motives, would serve the nation better by continuing their education."

Fordham immediately formed its own unit and enlisted enough applicants to make up four military companies and one naval company, some 500 men. Drills, bayonet practice and calisthenics became a regular part of campus life and a number of buildings were altered to accommodate the troops. Captain Robert W. Milburn was promoted to Major and made Commandant.

Student soldiers were paid $30 per month and the university received $1 a day for food, lodging and tuition. Those students who excelled were able to join the Officers Training Corps.

With encampments set up on campus by the War Department, the army was said to have "occupied Rose Hill," turning the scenic campus into a military training center. The soldiers in command went so far as to demand changes to the curriculum. The Jesuits complied, adapting their philosophy and science courses to war subjects and radio theory; they were told to drop classical courses. Some soldiers and sailors made it onto the football team.

According to the book, *Fordham University School of Law: A History*, by Robert J. Kaczorowski, Fordham Law students, during the fall of 1917, sold $15,500 in Liberty Bonds toward the New York Federal Reserve District campaign to raise $1.5 billion of the national goal of $3.8 billion.

Once the Armistice came on November 11, 1919, Fordham jumped at the War Department's invitation to disband the SATC.

In the end, Fordham students and alumni comprised three Major-Generals, two Colonels, one Lieutenant-Colonel, four Majors, 20 Captains, 10 Chaplains, around 90 First Lieutenants and 50 Second Lieutenants. And that was just the Army.

Thirty-six students lost their lives overseas.

The war, tragically, is also said to have cost the university its president. Fr. Mulry, whom President Wilson had appointed as a member of the Advisory Council of National Defense, is reported to have thrown all his physical and "oratorical" energies into the war effort. He traveled about giving patriotic speeches, conducting soldiers' missions and holding Mass for the troops.

One day, preaching at Fort Dix in New Jersey, he was quoted as saying: "Every face I saw in a day's journey through the camp was a pleasant one; there wasn't a long face among the thousands I looked into."

While celebrating another Mass at the military installation, he said, "I have not patience with the pacifists and conscientious objectors who too often throw over their selfish cowardice the cloak of religious principle. We all hate war and we all love peace, but we cannot and we must not enjoy a peace with dishonor. Our splendid American manhood demands war rather than peace at such a price. Go over there and take the trenches that your brothers are holding for you. Victory will come. God wills it!"

According to Edward P. Gilleran's "The Life of Father Mulry," in the *Fordham Monthly*, "One Sunday morning, before a meeting of the Alumni Sodality, his physician, with a grave face, told some of us who knew Father Mulry well that he was a sick man and asked us to urge him to go away for a rest. The Rector [Mulry] laughed at the suggestion when the men made it. 'Just a biliousness,' he said. And he lit his cigar and sat down at his desk for another day of work.

"In January 1919 Father Mulry's condition made it imperative for the Jesuit Provincial to insist on his withdrawing from the Presidency of Fordham. Then followed the illness, which had been coming over him for months. He died August 31, 1921."

In its obituary of Father Mulry, *The New York Times* wrote that he had resigned from Fordham to enter war work in France and that his resignation was only accepted after two attempts, but there's no evidence he ever made it to France. According to the

Times, "So anxious was he to go to the front that he offered to contribute $5,000 a year toward the salary of his successor."

A footnote, long forgotten from Father Mulry's reign was his move to allow women to matriculate at Fordham Law School, which he did in 1918 after lengthy discussions with the faculty and its hierarchy.

At long last, in 1918, Fordham students started a weekly newspaper that was deemed acceptable by the administration. *The Ram* was launched in conjunction with a journalism program that years later became one of the most prominent in the U.S. The university took the right path by introducing a practical program that would teach the basics of journalism and how to actually put together a newspaper. (Radio, television and the Web were still decades away.) It included lectures from visiting newspaper reporters and editors who lectured to the students.

The Ram started out as a simple letter sent to the Fordham students serving abroad in the war, but became a weekly on February 7, 1918. It was believed to be the first weekly newspaper at a Catholic university in the eastern part of the U.S. (As noted earlier, the *Goose-Quill* of the mid-19th century was not allowed to be printed.)

According to Father Gannon's book, the first *Ram* editor-in-chief, Paul T. O'Keefe, class of 1919, told the founding story years later to a Ram reporter:

The second edition of the Ram published.

"This whole ugly tradition began back in the early fall months of 1917. A journalism course had been started that year. There were a lot of Fordham men overseas, a good many of them in the Fordham Ambulance Corps. We decided that they'd like to hear of Fordham so we made them guinea pigs. At first we were going to put out a mimeographed sheet, but later grew reckless and went out for the Pulitzer Prize with an eight-page edition. Twenty-three of us, mostly juniors, set to work, sold ads and somehow managed to get the paper together. On February 7, 1918, the first Fordham Ram appeared and a new era in American journalism was begun!"

"Only one of the first editorial staff ever took up writing. His name was Matthew Taylor and he was circulation manager. Eleven of the original staff members are lawyers. Three of them are dead and one of them hasn't been heard of since graduation. Another, Denis Blake, became a priest, and the rest are now statisticians, contractors, court librarians, doctors, and automotive dealers."

The IRT Jerome Avenue Line of the New York City Subway opened a few blocks west of the Grand Concourse in 1917. This spurred a housing boom for upwardly mobile, predominantly Jewish and Italian families, who were then able to leave the crowded tenement buildings of Manhattan behind. Development of the Concourse was furthered when the IND line reached the Concourse in 1933. By the mid-1930s, almost 300 apartment buildings had been built along the boulevard. Many had wide courtyards with grass and shrubs. The buildings had great detailing, like gargoyles, intricate iron doors and huge windows. The nicest among them are some of the finest examples of Art Deco and Art Moderne architecture in the U.S.

Another high note marking the latter part of the decade at Fordham was the arrival (though he soon departed) of "The Fordham Flash," a baseball player named Frank Frisch. From the class of 1920, Frisch came to Fordham in 1916 as a scrappy, Bronx-born 165-pound infielder and one of the fastest base runners of his time. A multi-talented athlete who also played football and basketball, and ran track, Frisch was the star of the baseball team, but was drafted by the New York Giants before graduation. Despite that, he was voted the person who had "Done Most for Fordham" by his class. In 1921, Frisch led the National League with 48 steals. After the Giants, he played for the St. Louis Cardinals and, following his playing days, served as manager of the Cardinals, Pittsburgh Pirates and Chicago Cubs. A legend to generations of Fordham fans, Frisch

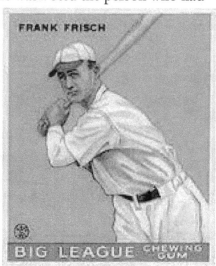

was elected to the Baseball Hall of Fame in 1947. He was also a broadcaster who did play-by-play for the Giants following his playing career, perhaps one of the first in a long line of successful Fordham alumni who became sportscasters. Frisch died following a Maryland car accident in 1973. In 1949, Ogden Nash had written the following poem for *Sport Magazine*: "F is for Fordham, and Frankie and Frisch; I wish he were back with the Giants, I wish."

Chapter V:
The Twenties Did Not Roar at Fordham

By 1920 the American economy began to get back on its feet, but that was not the case at Fordham. There was the unfortunate closing of the medical school (with the unfounded hope that it would reopen at some point in the future). And, there was hope there would be expansion under the new, young president, Edward P. Tivnan, S.J., a chemistry professor and former regent of the Fordham Medical School, who was just 37 years old. But, the debt kept mounting and Tivnan initiated a fundraising drive for $1.9 million. $1.4 million was to be used to further existing schools and programs and $500,000 would be put toward the endowment that Fordham lacked.

The endowment was supposed to fund scholarships to help students afford the tuition that was

From the 1920 Freshman Rule Book

1. Every Freshman must know his rules by heart; also the "Fordham Ram."
2. Freshman must always carry matches for upper-classmen.
3. Freshmen must move off the sidewalks to allow upper-classmen to pass. (Rule applies only when on campus).
4. Freshmen must wear hats prescribed by the Sophomores, on the campus and within one block of the campus.
5. Freshmen must wear black ties and socks on campus.
6. At any gathering of upperclassmen, Freshmen must perform as they are commanded.
7. Freshmen must tip their hats to Seniors while on campus.
8. Freshmen must wear regulation hats, ties, and socks at all athletic functions whether played at home or away.
9. No freshman is allowed to wear any insignia of any former school.
10. Freshmen cannot smoke in the presence of an upper-classman, without the permission of the upper-classman, on the campus.

A series of three football games will be played between the Freshmen and the Sophomores. If the Freshmen should win two games, Rule 10 will be modified.

then $110 per year, though the average student paid just $55. Father Tivnan said at the time, "We fortunately do not face a great budget for professional salaries. Jesuit teachers find their reward in terms other than money. With a few exceptions, our faculty and administrative force labor for the pure love of serving God."

A fundraiser was hired, then fired, and the job to procure the needed funds was handed over to an alumnus, Edward P. Gilleran, class of 1913. There was a fundraising dinner, again at the Waldorf, an appeal to alumni and other solicitations. In the end only $157,000 was raised.

Still, the university expanded by adding the School of Accounting, today known as The Gabelli School of Business, which opened in Manhattan in 1920. In 1923, a one-year evening pre-law course was instituted and extended to a two-year program a few years later.

At the campus in the Bronx, changes were made in 1921 to the academic curriculum when the "departmental system" was adopted. Per a meeting of Jesuits from around the country, at least eight departments were to be established at each of their colleges. Teachers would be restricted to teaching one subject, though they would have to teach several classes. And there would be fewer class hours and more preparation on the part of students. This meant a departure from the heavy emphasis on Latin, Greek and philosophy. Greek would henceforth be an elective.

Science programs would be strengthened. Father Tivnan, who had spent at least a year in charge of the seismic station when he was a scholastic in 1910, was in favor of beefing up the science curriculum.

Finally, high schools would be separated from colleges, hence the annexation of Fordham Preparatory School into its own entity. (There was in fact a years-long movement to get rid of the preparatory school altogether.)

The landscape at Rose Hill changed as well. There was a new iron fence encircling the campus border. A number of its pillars near the Third Avenue gate served as a World War I memorial to commemorate the 36 Fordham students who gave their lives. Dedicated on November 14, 1920, Generals John Pershing, Robert Lee Bullard and Clarence (Edward's Parade) Edwards were on hand. Eleven tennis courts with a clubhouse were constructed. St. John's Hall, then a dorm for seniors, was completely renovated and remodeled.

The present Murray-Weigel Hall was built in 1922, though it was first named for the Messenger of the Sacred Heart. In 1965, it was converted into a residence for Jesuit scholastics commemorating two New York Jesuit theologians prominent in the days of Vatican II, John Courtney Murray and Gustav Weigel.

Photo: Fordham Archives

Even though Father Tivnan wanted to build a new library, pressure to support athletics prevailed and construction of a new $400,000 gym was planned instead. The

The Rose Hill Gym in its early days. Edwards Parade (right foreground) was still a football field.

24,000-square-foot, 1,100-person capacity building, with a basketball court and basement swimming pool, that stands today across from Edward's Parade, was dedicated on January 16, 1924. It was a boon to the basketball program, which finally had a place of its own to practice and compete with other schools. From 1924 to 1927, the team had winning seasons and, in 1927-28, it won the Eastern Collegiate Championship.

One of Father Tivnan's greatest challenges stemmed from the money-losing Fordham football team of these years. Even

89

though the team finished with more wins than losses in the first 20 years of the 20th century, including an undefeated season in 1918 – and had a number of All-American players – it was costing a great deal because athletes were paid to play. The university was quietly disregarding NCAA regulations. There were even reports that students who had been expelled from school were still playing on the football team.

According to *The Fordham Monthly*, "hired 'athletes' were less conspicuous on the gridiron last fall. Strange as it may seem to the initiated, college students are now actually beginning to partake in college athletics! [But] college athletics is a misnomer. There is no such animal in the scholastic zoo. Every college has its football and baseball teams, most of the players being hired for their athletic proficiency. This small group, which does not need the training at all, gets all the training. The student body, which stands pre-eminently in need of training gets none."

A Fordham University Athletic Council made up of alumni was appointed. They were to control the direction of all athletic activities.

The NCAA began to crack down on "scholarships." Fordham had 69 listed in the 1920-21 Treasurer's report. In a letter to the NCAA, responding to a directive he had received, Father Tivnan, who like many of those at the top who claim ignorance to situations under their own noses, wrote the following:

"I also am of the opinion that many colleges and universities have neglected the provisions of the [NCAA] resolution. It would not be fair to specify, because I am not in possession of facts. But it does look rather strange to find men playing on certain teams until the end of the season, in football, for example, and then learn that they disappear from the scene armed with a 'war-diploma' or some other such meaningless document. Sport for sport's sake has no place in the college curriculum and unless linked with the intellectual training which we, as educators, profess to give, will be productive only of harm."

The alumni-headed athletic council was soon dissolved and the university was back in control. Father Tivnan wrote that Fordham was still undergoing a tough time financially, but that sports would be cleaned up:

"The situation today...is really worse than it was when we began the experiment...now there is indebtedness running into the thousands. There has been chaos with regard to the registration of students. We did not know what students were or were not registered. There are students in the Law School who have been most irregular in attendance and who have paid no attention to studies and in consequence there is great dissatisfaction among the members of the faculty. Students have been forbidden to play because of the poor scholastic showing they made, indeed, have been dismissed from the school and yet we found them playing on the teams...

"Again, the matter of finances, we were to be relieved of all burden and yet, the burden has become greater than before. In addition, our credit has suffered materially with several houses and this has thrown a shadow over the reputation which we have always had of paying our bills promptly..."

In another communiqué to a colleague, Tivnan later wrote: "We shall undoubtedly have many lean years in the matter of victories, but they will be clean years."

The athletics department was reorganized and football continued under a new coach, Frank Gargan, class of 1911. Surprisingly, the team did not fall on its face. The 1925-26 season was a winning one with eight victories and one loss, to Georgetown, though fans and supporters were disappointed because the schedule had been an easy one.

Team sports may have been rescued by a man whose name is almost as familiar to the Fordham community as that of Clarence Edwards. John F. "Jack" Coffey, class of 1910, for whom today's football stadium is named, was known as the "Silver Fox." Coffey was a shortstop and football player who went on

91

to play professional baseball for the Detroit Tigers and Boston Red Sox, becoming the only person in major league history to play with Ty Cobb and Babe Ruth in the same season. Coffey returned to Fordham as a winning baseball coach after his playing

Photo: Fordham Athletics

Jack Coffey in his playing days.

career. In 1926, he was made Graduate Manager of Athletics. Famous for his gift with people, Coffey was the consummate PR man before public relations was a profession. He was proficient in Latin and Greek and fluent in French, German, Spanish and Italian. He remembered everyone's name and was able to forge relationships in the sports world throughout the country. Under his leadership, which lasted officially until his retirement in 1958, and unofficially until his death in 1966, Coffey was the face and personality of Fordham sports. *Ram* sportswriter Caswell Adams wrote, "There hasn't been a Fordham man, bookworm, crapshooter or athlete who hasn't felt the influence of Jack."

In 1924, there was a change of command again at the university when the Jesuits transferred Father Tivnan to Weston College in Massachusetts, where he would oversee training for the order's priests. The new president, Rev. William J. Duane, was installed on August 31, 1924. Considerably older than Tivnan at age 57, Duane had a lot more experience; he had been Prefect of Studies at Woodstock College. Father Duane was fortunate to have come at a time when the financial troubles at

Fordham were abating. There was a more robust enrollment and the use of part-time teachers was saving the university money. By the time he was gone, there was no debt and the number of students in the entire university was 9,326, with 1,322 in Fordham College. He added five buildings to the campus, most designed by the architect who designed the gym, Emile G. Perrot, and worked further to put the athletic program back on its feet.

Duane was able to complete Father Tivnan's dream of building a new library. Completed in 1926, Duane Library may have seemed cramped, labyrinth and lacking in space to later generations, but it was quite advanced for the 1920's and few would argue that its beauty was unmatched. Thousands of students from the 20's until the turn of the next century would spend hours holed up in its nooks and crannies, reading, studying and getting to know other classmates, particularly after the 1960's when women first studied at Rose Hill. The fact that it was a setting for the 1970 movie *Love Story* made it that much more romantic. The Old English structure had plenty of room for the university's 90,000-volume collection of books, and with its beautiful carved wood work and stained glass windows, was welcomed with open arms when it was finally dedicated by Bishop John J. Dunn in 1927. *The Woodstock Letters* reported, "Students of the Inquisition will…be elated when they find that the famous Migne collection may be found on the shelves of the library very soon."

Begun in 1926, Larkin Hall (named for the 1851-54 president, John Larkin, S.J.) on Fordham Road was also dedicated during Father Duane's reign to be used as the home of the biology department. Science Hall was rededicated as Freeman Hall, home to the physics department. In 1928, Loyola Hall (named for St. Ignatius Loyola, founder of the Society of Jesus) was built to house the Jesuits. A huge celebration was held on April 7, 1929 to mark the reopening of the University Church after an expansion and renovation of its interior, including the addition of the gothic dome, two side chapels with altars and seating to accommodate 1,150 people, triple the previous number.

Of Larkin Hall, the *Fordham Monthly* said at the time:

"This magnificent edifice deserves a separate paragraph. It represents the highest degree of perfection in the building craft. To recite its features would occupy a volume alone…Its architecture is of the old English type so perfectly shown in the library, and follows the grey and white stone pattern.

"Its laboratories are most extensive and complete in their equipment. There is a microscopic laboratory with microtomes built in the tables; there is even space for live animals which may be kept for the aid of biologists."

A biology student, Dr. James Forbes, class of 1932, and later a professor of biology, remembered Father Joseph Assmuth, who taught biology and zoology. "When he crossed the threshold, the class arose as one! He waved us down and began talking. He was in full charge until he dismissed the class after the bell rang. He spoke with a slight German accent, but he enunciated his words clearly. Scientific words were written on the blackboard and their roots were explained.

"During the first class meeting, when the course organization was explained together with all the dos and don'ts, we were told that the class examinations were Blitzes, unannounced flashes of lightning that would last five minutes – no more. When a blitz was planned, Assmuth entered the room, he announced 'Blitz!' He took a time-clock set for five minutes from the pocket of his lab coat and set it on the lecture table. Mullen (Dr. Mullen, his assistant) would uncover the paper, half-sheets of mimeograph paper, and pass out the paper along the front row to be passed back.

"The questions were simple and direct. When the questions were read, the clock was started. While you were trying to put your thoughts into a lucid answer, the clock was ticking the time away! When the bell rang at the end of the time, pencils and pens were raised, and the papers were passed to the center aisle of the room. Woe to the student who tried to dot an i or cross a t! At the next lecture, or so, he would come in with a clip-board and read out the names of those who had 'fallen in battle,' the failures, those who had done very well, and finally the one to whom the laurel wreath was given, the one who got the top grade. Grades, however, were never given out. Assmuth said he never failed a student, he gave 100 percent to all his students, but the grade the student took was up to him!"

An-other student of that era, Dr. John

Collins, class of 1930, who went on to become a history professor, remembered how small Fordham was, so small students could not escape the gaze of teachers and administrators. "Father Deane, the dean of students, could look out his window in the Administration Building and if he saw a student walking on the quadrangle, he would come out and ask, 'why aren't you in class?'"

In concert with those watchful eyes, there was a crackdown on socializing as Prohibition hit the U.S. A gala Junior Prom that was held each year at the famous Biltmore Hotel near Grand Central Terminal in Manhattan was a favorite among students; it was known as the biggest social occasion of a student's four years. When there was an incident at a similar event at another Catholic College, Cardinal Hayes banned such proms at all Catholic colleges in the Archdiocese of New York, his domain.

The 1932 kidnapping and murder of Charles A. Lindbergh, Jr. should have had nothing whatsoever to do with Fordham University, but alas there was a retired professor and tennis coach, Dr. John Francis Condon, who became an integral part of the incident and the subsequent prosecution of Bruno Richard Hauptmann for the crime. (Condon had also received a Master's degree from Fordham in 1902.)

At the time of the Lindbergh abduction, Dr. Condon was 72 years old and living on Decatur Avenue, not far from Fordham. He spent some of his spare time writing to the editor of the local newspaper, the *Bronx Home News*. Deeply troubled by the plight of the Lindberghs, Dr. Condon wrote an open letter to the kidnappers and offered to act as an intermediary.

His letter was published in the paper's March 8, 1932 edition. The following evening, Dr. Condon received a letter from the culprits – a letter authenticated by the same pattern of interlocking circles found on the ransom note left in the Lindbergh nursery. It read:

Mr. Condon

We trust you, but we will note come in your hous it is to danger. even you can note know if Police or secret servise is watching you follow this instruction.

Take a car and drive to the last supway station from jerome Ave here. 100 feet from this last station on the left seide is a empty frankfurther stand with a big open Porch around, you will find a notise in senter of the porch underneath a stove. this notise will tell you were to find us. act accordingly. After 3/4 of a houer be on the place, bring the mony with you.

The Lindberghs subsequently authorized Dr. Condon to act on their behalf. A series of communications between "Jafsie" – a moniker for Dr. Condon derived from his initials: J. F. C. – and "John" – the self-professed identity of one of the kidnappers – ensued. Jafsie met with John twice during the ransom negotiations: first to ascertain the welfare of the child and later to deliver the ransom money. Both meetings took place in cemeteries.

Given his face-to-face contacts with the kidnapper, Dr. Condon was a key witness for the prosecution; he was the only one who could identify "John." At trial in 1935 he did so. In the Flemington, New Jersey courtroom, Dr. Condon unequivocally identified Bruno Richard Hauptmann as "the individual with whom he had met and to whom he had given the ransom money." Without Dr. Condon's testimony, the state's case against Hauptmann would have been greatly weakened and, perhaps, Hauptmann would not have gone to the electric chair. Some, as lead defense counsel Edward Reilly argued on cross-examination, believed that Dr. Condon himself was involved in the kidnapping. In his later years, Dr. Condon authored a memoir of the affair titled: *Jafsie Tells All.* (As most know, Charles Lindbergh, Jr.'s body was found a short distance from the Lindbergh home two months after his abduction.)

During Father Duane's tenure, the Administration Building actually caught fire – twice, in 1924 and in 1928. On one of those occasions, Dean Michael Jessup, a Jesuit, who ran to the aid of others and tried to save records, sustained serious injury. The university was said to have done well by the insurance settlement.

The next year, there was a soon-to-be world famous commencement speaker, the newly elected Governor of New York State, who received an honorary Doctor of Laws. A graduating student, Tom Quinn remembered, "The day of our graduation, I saw a beautiful open Packard pull up to the college and a gentleman, with a little assistance, got out and got up, and he gave the speech of the occasion for our graduation. I was very much impressed and said 'That man will go far.' It's one of the few occasions in my life I've ever been right, and I can't forget it. His name was Franklin D. Roosevelt."

Roosevelt, accompanied by his wife, Eleanor, and their daughter, Anna Eleanor Dall, spoke that day about the spiritual meaning of the word, Excelsior, contained in the New York State motto. "To live up to that great motto in its right interpretation," he said, "should be the goal of our state. To think of that motto in its spiritual aspect, to think of it in connection with our duty to our fellow men, to think of it in the light of the Golden Rule, will mean that the 12 million people, who by the grace of God, chance to be citizens of the human political unit known as the State of New York, will in the days to come measure up more widely and more truly to the highest teachings of religion and to the best purposes of our American civilization.

"One of the greatest privileges which I have had in connection with civic service has been the chance which it has given me to get to know the United States as a whole. It is true that many people in other parts of the country do not understand the higher purposes of the State of New York, but it is also true that some of us in the State of New York are not sufficiently understanding of the higher aims and purposes of our fellow citizens in other parts of the nation.

"In the final analysis, there is much of truth in the thought that one cannot hate a person whom one knows. Most prejudice is founded on ignorance; most wrong thinking and most dislike is on the part of those who are strangers."

It was the first of two visits Roosevelt is known to have made to Rose Hill. More on the second visit later on.

Father Duane also oversaw the opening of satellite campuses called "extension centers" in Mount Vernon, New Rochelle, Yonkers, Hoboken, Fort Lee, Jersey City and Newark where courses leading to various degrees were offered. And, he returned the military to Fordham. The cadet corps, which had disappeared after World War I, was reignited as ROTC. The *Fordham Monthly* wrote about the joy felt when almost half of all students signed up:

"It is no difficult task for the old timers to remember the days when the Cadet Corps at Fordham was the pride and glory of the little college on Rose Hill...Today only a few faded photographs that used to hang in Alumni Hall recall the martial splendor of those times. Since then, with the exception of a year or two during the war, there has been no military activity of any sort on the campus. The spirit of militarism, like the other old landmarks about the place, seemed to have passed away to a quiet obscurity – and then, the Resurrection! A branch of Reserve Officers Training Corps has been established here for instruction in Coast Artillery. The battalions of old are to march again! Gone, perhaps, are the spiked helmets and the uniforms of yesterday, but the lines of Fordham men are once more to sweep across the campus in the old formations, as their fathers did before them..."

Chapter VI:
The Great Depression and
the Pre-War Years

As the Great Depression took root, Fordham again had a new president, Father Aloysius J. Hogan, 39, who was originally from Philadelphia and had a Ph.D. in philosophy from Cambridge in Great Britain. In 1930, when he took office, football was surging and enrollment was up to more than 9,000 (1,322 in the College), and there was no debt.

But academics were actually slipping. Fordham did not make the list of schools approved by the American Council on Education (ACE). Among the strikes against it were that teachers were not publishing enough and the library was not considered top notch. In addition, Fordham was considered to be awarding too many advanced degrees relative to its number of students and the number who were studying only part-time. According to the Jesuit publication *America*, "Fordham had slipped into 'intellectual inertia.'" In addition, the Association of American Universities (AAU) dropped Fordham from its list of approved colleges.

Whether for good or not is open to debate, but during this time the Jesuits imposed a somewhat standardized curriculum through formation of the Jesuit Educational Association. It would move the academic side of the Jesuit colleges still farther away from the study of Latin, Greek, theology and philosophy and more toward the humanities and sciences, in keeping with other American universities. Out west, the new Jesuit universities being formed were teaching nothing resembling the classics since the student bodies of those regions would not have been interested and probably would not have enrolled if classics courses were offered. Of course, the old guard didn't like this one bit, including Father Hogan who told the faculty at the time:

"We refuse to be stampeded into following the pseudo-educational vagaries of experimentalists, whether they advocate the abolition of substantial educational procedure or advise the introduction of some whimsical fad. We refuse to fore-go our time-proven, permanent, unassailable principles and ideals of true education because of the formalistic, purely extrinsic requirements of the so-called standardizing agencies, which are cramping and maiming our educational activity in America today. Their undemocratic methods tend to destroy that initiative and spontaneity so essential to true education. Moreover, their ever-varying and purely arbitrary requirements are indicative of the instability of their whole purpose and aim."

Hogan even went so far as to issue a formal protest against the

Photos: Fordham Archives (l) and Gary Wayne Gilbert (r)

Keating Hall and Gasson Hall at Boston College bear a striking resemblance to each other, thanks to Father Hogan.

new program, though eventually it was instituted.

A traditionalist, Hogan told the graduating class of 1932, "What we need in this country today is more selflessness and less selfishness in our national life, in our business world, in our social activities, in our individual lives. We need, yes, we sorely need in America today a speedy return to the principles of Jesus Christ, so clearly reiterated in the Encyclical of Our Holy Father, Pope Pius XI."

With visions that Fordham should have a statelier look, like those he admired while studying at Cambridge and Boston

College, Father Hogan conceived the idea of the quadrangle that is now Edward's Parade, which had previously been an athletic field. He paved the path around its perimeter and bordered the grass with the cedar posts that remain in the 21st century.

Again in the tradition of the universities abroad, Hogan decided that Fordham needed a trademark building, even though there was not enough money to build one. With inspiration from Gasson Hall at Boston College, $300,000 of the university's cash and another $200,000 he was able to borrow, Hogan began construction of Keating Hall. It took a number of years to finish, even though materials at that time were inexpensive and there was a more-than-willing workforce available. The ultimate cost, according to Father Gannon, was $1.3 million.

With its medieval style, four Gothic turrets and the grand central clock tower reaching into the sky, Keating is truly a hallmark of the campus. It was designed specifically so that the steps and the western front would provide a backdrop for future commencement exercises with the afternoon sun behind the audience to light the speakers. Comprising 36,000 square feet and forming a perfect square with each side being 200 feet long, it is named after Fordham Treasurer Joseph Keating, S.J. (1910-1948). The building was designed by New York City architect Robert J. Reiley who intended that it resemble St. John's Hall, the first of Archbishop Hughes' structures. Built with a huge first floor auditorium, the Blue Chapel and a cafeteria, the building later became home to radio station WFUV. The tower that long supported the WFUV antenna (and was almost excised from the plans due to cost) rises 90 feet above the roof. The building was dedicated on December 6, 1936, after Father Hogan had left.

Keating now has smart classrooms, a media center and language labs, but maintains the central meditative area on the first floor made of crab orchard stone that makes it reminiscent of an old cathedral and retains just about all its original charm. In the past 75 years, Keating has been the location for the filming

102

of a number of famous movies, including Quiz Show (1994) directed by Robert Redford and A Beautiful Mind (2001) with Russell Crow. Both were nominated for Oscars; the latter was a winner.

Hogan's main focus, unhappily for the athletics department, was football. He is known to have tried to micromanage the team, which nonetheless had its most heralded decade before or since. Jack Coffey continued to be in charge of the athletics program and there was a new football coach, Francis William "Cav" Cavanaugh, a World War I vet who had earned the nickname, "The Iron Major." Cavanaugh came from Dartmouth and Boston College (then considered a much smaller school than Fordham) and led the team in 1929 to its first undefeated season. From 1930 to 1931 there was only one loss, though sports was still losing money.

Photo: Fordham Athletics
Vince Lombardi at Fordham.

The football team ultimately benefited when Cavanaugh was forced to resign in 1932, due to illness brought on by injuries sustained in the Great War. He was replaced by "Sleepy" Jim Crowley from Notre Dame who had been one of Knute Rockne's star players from the famed "Four Horsemen." Paid the huge sum (for those days) of $11,000 per year, Crowley delivered bona fide fame to the Fordham football program because he was responsible for the infamous "Seven Blocks of Granite," the team's defensive line. (It actually included up to 12 players over

103

the years, though the credited names are John Druze, Al Babartsky Vincent Lombardi, Alex Wojciechowicz, Nat Pierce, Ed Franco and Leo Paquin.) One student athlete of the time, John M. Canella, class of 1930, contended the name had been bandied about as early as *his* playing days, but said it didn't take hold until Crowley became coach.

Like Rockne, Crowley was known for his rousing locker room pep talks. He ended up with a record of 56 wins, 13 losses and seven ties from 1932 to 1941.

Of course, the star among the "Seven Blocks" was the storied Vince Lombardi. Most readers of this book will know that the Brooklyn-born Lombardi went on to become a coach at Fordham and later coach of the Green Bay Packers from 1959 to 1967. He was named NFL Coach of the Year (1959) and a member of the Pro Football Hall of Fame (1971), not to mention the most famous member of the Fordham University Hall of Fame (1970).

Lombardi, whose life has been chronicled in David Maraniss' *When Pride Still Mattered*, and in the Broadway play, "Lombardi" (2010-11), was at first planning to become a priest. He began high school in the seminary, but transferred to Brooklyn's St. Francis Prep, then graduated magna cum laude from Fordham in 1937. He actually started law school while working for a finance company during the day, but was then recruited by a New Jersey high school to take an assistant coaching position. From there he returned to Fordham to coach (1947) and went on to West Point (1949) and finally the pros – the New York Giants and the Packers, where he led the team to victory in Super Bowls I and II.

While conventional wisdom has long had it that Lombardi originated the phrase, "Winning isn't everything, it's the only thing," that quote was actually borrowed from UCLA Bruins football coach Henry Russell (Red) Sanders. What Lombardi said for himself was, "Winning is not a sometime thing, it is an all the time thing. You don't do things right once in a while…you do them right all the time."

At Fordham, Maraniss attributes two stories to Lombardi that personify his aggressiveness. One has it that he retaliated against a Jesuit who referred to the athletes as "hogs on the way to the trough" by crushing a buttered piece of bread on the priest's bald head while making his way out of the dining hall. Even worse, he knocked the teeth out of a guy at a sorority dance who had called him "the little Guinea." He was also known for being suspended from Fordham when he struck a fellow player who called him a "wop."

There's no doubt Lombardi learned a lot about leadership and morality, if not grace, from the Jesuits at Fordham. Another quote attributed to him is: "Morally, the life of the organization must be of exemplary nature. This is one phase where the organization must not have criticism."

He is also quoted as saying, "Leadership is based on a spiritual quality – the power to inspire, the power to inspire others to follow… Leadership rests not only upon ability, not only upon capacity – having the capacity to lead is not enough. The leader must be willing to use it. His leadership is then based on truth and character. There must be truth in the purpose and will power in the character."

Edward P. Gilleran, Jr., class of 1947 and a sports editor of *The Ram* quoted Assistant Coach Frank Leahy as saying Fordham athletes were distinguished by the belief that, "We were a different breed in those bygone days. We played sports for the glory of our school and for personal achievement. That was all there was to it, but it was enough for us."

Chapter VII:
Marching Towards World War II
The University Turns 100

When Father Robert Ignatius Gannon became president in 1936, he would make monumental changes at Fordham and would have the longest tenure of any single president up until that time – 13 years. Gannon was a Georgetown-educated New Yorker of means who had been to Europe multiple times as a young man and had actually had an audience with Pope Pius X. He had attended receptions at the White House as a Georgetown student, had met President Taft and went on to become dean of St. Peter's College in Jersey City, by then a training ground for the Jesuit leaders who often ended up in the Fordham hierarchy. He was

Photo: Fordham Archives

Robert Ignatius Gannon, S.J.

actually born on Staten Island in 1893, which led many to crow that his erudition and perceived snobbery were at least somewhat disingenuous.

When Gannon was made president, Fordham's numbers were good – 8,000 students (1,600 in Fordham College), 641 faculty members and property valued at more than $8 million. But, there was still a poor academic standing and outstanding debts associated with construction of Keating Hall. Interestingly, at this time there were only 53 Jesuits teaching at Fordham, just 8% of the faculty.

Gannon, by his own admission, first hired a public relations firm. He then began a successful attempt to regain the AAU rating that had eluded Fordham in the preceding years.

According to Philip Gleason's *Contending with Modernity: Catholic Higher Education in the Twentieth Century*, "He acted decisively to concentrate graduate work (and the library resources needed to support it) on the Bronx campus, where a faculty, soon to be strengthened by distinguished refugee scholars, devoted itself exclusively to graduate work in a newly constructed graduate [Keating] hall. The initiation of these improvements, along with downsizing the undergraduate student body and making it more academically select (enrollment was cut from 1,620 to 1,200 in the College), moved the AAU to restore Fordham to its collegiate list within months of Gannon's taking office, and to accord it recognition as a 'university of complex organization' a few years later."

Gannon vehemently resisted calls to raise money by increasing enrollment and did the opposite. He said: "Since the enrollment of the ideal college is limited by the power of the institution to give each student the intellectual, religious and social advantages implied in a liberal education – specifically a degree of personal attention sufficient to break down a crowd in to a group of persons – we felt it our duty to reduce the number of undergraduates on the campus. After careful study it was determined that we were not doing our best with 1,620, but we could achieve good results with a body of about 1,200. As this meant the elimination of the lowest quarter, it was a major operation calling for time and care. Thus far, more than 200 of the less apt have been diverted into other fields and we hope in another year to reach our goal."

The new chief administrator expanded the theater and communications programs. He initiated an honors program and instituted a guidance program for students. He was unsuccessful, however, at establishing a Fordham chapter of Phi Beta Kappa. That would come in 1958.

Gannon decided that the teaching staff needed improving. He took advantage of the many European academics who were fleeing the continent. Among the respected faculty members he delivered to the university was historian Dr. Victor Hess, discoverer of the cosmic ray and a 1936 Nobel Prize winner in physics who taught physics at Fordham for 25 years. He was also able to retain historian Oscar Heleck from the University of Warsaw, sociologist Nicholas Timashef from St. Petersburg, Dietrich von Hildebrand, a philosopher from Germany and Hilaire Belloc, an English essayist, historian, novelist, journalist and poet who was in residence in the history department. From NYU, he hired Ross Hoffman, a European historian.

To continue to attract talent, Gannon was able to raise salaries and make it easier for professors to become tenured. Assistant professors during the late 30's could expect to make upwards of $3,000 per year. Tuition was raised at about the same time from $200 to $250 per term.

Said Gannon, "The President was no longer exposed to the embarrassment of private arguments about money or promotion, and the faculty members could plan for the future with confidence." He noted that he felt he would then be able to compete with other schools to retain teachers with the best credentials.

The professors also benefited when he began to procure research grants – and research – for the university.

After many years of being left out of the study abroad programs that had sprung up at other institutions, Fordham finally got into the game during the summer of 1939 when 15 students traveled to Grenoble, France. Once in Europe, they also visited the Pope's summer residence at Castel Gandolfo, where Pope Pius XII – the former Cardinal Eugenio Pacelli – received them and remembered an earlier visit to Fordham. It must have been quite a moment for those young Catholic men in that era.

As alluded to earlier, now that Keating Hall was built, Father Gannon had a huge, new, empty building to fill. He announced that a number of the graduate schools would move into the new building, allowing the university to consolidate to a great extent. Gannon thought the consolidation would increase the number of undergrads who went on to graduate school, as the shift would create a more seamless transition for students who could complete their undergraduate work and move into grad school without switching locations. It worked. He was able to increase enrollment in the graduate schools, which surprised many who believed relocating them out of Manhattan would be a liability. The change also meant that after almost 30 years, Fordham would no longer have a presence in the Woolworth Building. As was his way, he staged an elaborate event, enlisting Cardinal Patrick Hayes to preside over the dedication.

Additionally, Gannon secured $210,000 from an anonymous donor to add the two wings to St. John's Hall – Robert's and Bishops' Halls – forming Queens Court in 1940. State of the art for the time, the new structures had private showers and a basement bowling alley. Bishops' was noted for its stained glass reproductions of the seals of the 18 bishops and cardinals in Fordham's history, placed in the windows of the main hall. Robert's Hall was named after Robert Cardinal Ballarmine, S.J., a noted figure in the Counter-Reformation of the Catholic Church, who was canonized in 1930 and named a Doctor of the Church.

Outdoors, there were upgrades to the landscape, with the planting of more than 1,800 new trees. Gannon introduced the Terrace of the Presidents, the granite steps leading up to Keating Hall. They would henceforth be engraved with the names of heads of state who visited. Among those so noted are George Washington, who visited Rose Hill Manor before it became St. John's College; Franklin Delano Roosevelt; Harry S. Truman; Richard Nixon; and various leaders from around the world.

A major player on the New York City speaking circuit during his day, Gannon set about on a fundraising mission, as would become his job and the job of many university presidents in the

20th century and beyond. He claimed to have raised millions of dollars per year for a number of years. Consistent with many

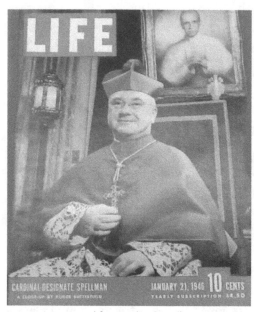

It was not unusual for Cardinal Spellman to grab headlines.

Catholics of the day, most notably his friend, Cardinal Francis J. Spellman, the Archbishop of New York who had succeeded Cardinal Hayes in 1939, his speeches were often strong anti-liberal, anti-Communist rants and pro-Franco/anti-British. Neither of the two priests was afraid to offend those who may have dared to disagree for fear of being denied donations.

Gannon and Spellman, a Fordham graduate (class of 1911 and a baseball player), were a team in many ways, who spent a great deal of time together plotting their separate, but sometimes mutual missions. Like Gannon, Spellman was an incredibly political religious leader and shared the university president's conservative, anti-communist beliefs. In fact, Gannon was later hand chosen by Spellman to be his official biographer.

As Spellman was a son of Fordham, his background is worth more than a few paragraphs.

According to a review in *The New York Times* of *The Life and Times of Francis Cardinal Spellman* by John Cooney, the headline of which was "Guileless and Machiavellian," writer William V. Shannon wrote that the Archbishop of New York (1939-1967)

was one of the most powerful and controversial figures of his time.

"In both the political and the ecclesiastical arenas, he sought power avidly and used it aggressively. He was the confidant, adviser and sometime agent of Presidents from Franklin D. Roosevelt to Lyndon B. Johnson. And he was influential in New York politics. As the Catholic military vicar to the American armed forces - a post separate from but complementary to his position as Archbishop – he supervised chaplains around the world and was a familiar visitor to battlefields during World War II and the wars in Korea and Vietnam."

In the book, Cooney wrote, "Spellman presented two distinct faces to the world. The one he wore most often in public was that of a cherubic, humble man who smiled often, spoke softly, and struck people as being not overly bright. The other face was that of a tough, demanding man who pushed hard, let little stand in his way, and ran roughshod over friend or foe to get what he wanted. His polar personalities shifted from guileless to Machiavellian." There were inevitable comparisons to Archbishop Hughes.

The review reported that Father Gannon praised the Cardinal at his 75th birthday dinner as "fearless, tireless, and shrewd . . . but at the same time . . . humble, whimsical, sentimental, incredibly thoughtful, supremely loyal, and, above all, a real priest."

Cooney also wrote, "For years rumors abounded about Cardinal Spellman being a homosexual. As a result many felt – and continue to feel – that Spellman the public moralist may well have been a contradiction of the man of the flesh."

"Spellman was the oldest son of a well-to-do grocer in Whitman, Massachusetts, a small town south of Boston. According to Cooney, "The harshness in his personality appears to have come from his dour father, to whom he was not close. In later life he often quoted in self-deprecating fashion his father's nasty advice: 'Son, always associate with people smarter than yourself, and that shouldn't be hard to do.'"

"His father's money enabled Spellman to have a better education and more chances for advancement in the church than if he had been a working-class boy attending a local seminary. Upon graduation from Fordham he spent five years at the North American College in Rome. Since he was a mediocre student, the education he received mattered less than opportunities Rome presented. He used his time there to ingratiate himself with important clerics in the Vatican Curia and wealthy American Catholic expatriates. These Roman connections proved crucial in his career.

"Returning to the Boston archdiocese in 1916, he spent nine years as a priest under the baleful eye of William Cardinal O'Connell, a tyrant of legendary proportions. Having taken an instant dislike to Spellman, O'Connell delighted in giving him a series of dusty assignments. Spellman, who had a volcanic temper, had to learn the practice of humility to survive. Rescued by well-placed friends in the Vatican, he returned to Rome for several years. Then, to O'Connell's dismay, the Pope named him Auxiliary Bishop of Boston in 1932.

Spellman's most important friend in Rome was Eugenio Pacelli, the future Pope Pius XII. It was an extraordinary stroke of good fortune that when the archbishopric of New York was vacant in the winter of 1938-39 and seemed about to be filled by another candidate, Pope Pius XI died. Once Pacelli was elected Pope, he appointed his friend to New York. Spellman would have been a prominent, but much less significant figure if, as expected, he had merely inherited O'Connell's job in Boston.

The Cooney book reports further that New York was most likely the richest diocese in the world, which meant that Spellman would have access to those of the highest rank and stature. As it was also the nation's financial center and the world media capital, "the front doors of the archbishop's residence opened into the heart of it. The job was made for a man such as Spellman."

Spellman was considered a success in his job by most measures. "A restless workaholic, he was a deft and forceful administrator, choosing able subordinates, cutting costs and negotiating advantageous real estate deals. Inheriting a huge debt, he proved a highly successful fundraiser." From 1955 to 1959, he spent $168 million building 15 churches, 94 schools, 22 rectories, 60 convents and 34 other institutions. Also a diplomat, he was credited with fostering relationships between the Vatican and American presidents.

"Why did he become such a bitterly controversial figure,?" asked Cooney. "Spellman was deeply reactionary in his theology and secular politics. He was, for example, hostile to ecumenism, liturgical reform (including saying the mass in English) and all intellectual attempts to take account of the truth that the church actually thrives in America's pluralistic and officially secular society. Instead, he belittled the separation of church and state as 'a shibboleth [a word or saying empty of real meaning].' He opposed First Amendment freedoms with the obsolete theory that 'error has no rights.'"

In American society as well as the Catholic Church (as Vatican II was to demonstrate in 1962-65), Spellman was moving against the tides of opinion and practice. The longer he wielded power, the more stubborn, opinionated and aggressive he became in trying to impose his views, and the wider the gap became between him and prevailing practice.

Somewhat of a turning point came for Spellman in 1949 when he broke a gravediggers strike by putting seminarians to work digging graves, while the union diggers were on the picket line. Many of the strikers, of course, were poorly paid Catholics. Later that same year, he attacked Eleanor Roosevelt for her opposition to federal aid for church-run schools. And, in 1951 he led a temporarily successful campaign to ban Roberto Rossellini's film

'The Miracle' in New York. All three incidents proved
disastrous. Later he publicly endorsed Senator Joseph
McCarthy's campaign against Communism. He also identified
himself and the church excessively with the Vietnam War.

Gannon and Spellman shared a love of publicity and a number
of beliefs and qualities. Many believe that for Gannon, his
temperament and strident viewpoints on the issues of the day are
the reason he is the only prominent president of the university
who does not have a building named after him.

Like Spellman and Hughes, Gannon was determined to make
Fordham a center of influence and to promote Catholicism.
Back in 1936, Gannon had hosted the future Pope Pius XII,
Cardinal Pacelli, then Cardinal Secretary of State. Later known
for remaining silent in public about the fate of the Jewish people
in Hitler's Germany, Pacelli was given a Doctor of Laws before
3,000 invited guests at Fordham. He made a speech to the
faculty on Keating Terrace and was serenaded by the 525-
member ROTC honor guard.

On another occasion, the president held a conference for the
nations of the Danube Valley, many of whom had very recently
been invaded by the Germans, calling it the Pax Romana
Congress.

Also in 1940, President Roosevelt's mother, Sarah Delano
Roosevelt, was invited to the Fordham campus to dedicate a
plaque to her second cousin, James Roosevelt Bayley, the
university's third president. It was a terribly raining day. Father
Gannon recalled later that he invited Mrs. Roosevelt back to his
office for a glass of sherry. He said the patrician Mrs. Roosevelt
answered the offer with, "For an awful moment I thought you
were going to suggest a cup of tea."

The class of 1940 was notable, as well. Among its members
were Peter A. Carlesimo, who became Fordham's athletic
director in 1968, Don McGannon, the future president of the
Westinghouse Corporation and Dick Breen, a famous Hollywood

attorney. Carlesimo, who sent 10 of his children to Fordham, remembered how strictly students were watched in those days. He said they had to be in their rooms by 7 p.m. They would study from 7:30 p.m. until 10 p.m., and only then could they turn on their radios. By 11:00 p.m., it was lights out and the Jesuits came around to make sure each man was tucked safely into bed.

Monday, October 28, 1940 may have been Fordham's biggest day ever. It was on that date that President Franklin Delano Roosevelt came to Rose Hill for a visit. He was the first sitting president to do so. (It was Roosevelt's second official appearance at Fordham; he had received an honorary LL.D. in 1929 when he was New York's governor.) This time the occasion was a campaign stop in his bid for reelection to a third term. Hard as it is to believe now, the president was running against Wendell Willkie, also a New Yorker and a Wall Street industrialist, who had visited Fordham for a football game. The Roosevelt campaign thought a Fordham stop for the president was also needed. Of course, that turned out not to be the case. Roosevelt won in a landslide and took all of New York State's 47 electoral votes.

Father Gannon had first asked that both the president and Willkie make a pair of nationally televised addresses while sharing the stage at Fordham, but the White House would have none of that.

The cover story for the president's visit was a Commander in Chief's review of the ROTC unit at Fordham, which had 525 members. Quite an exhibition was staged for Roosevelt. The president's motorcade was greeted by throngs of supporters as it made its way to Fordham by way of the Grand Concourse. Once on campus, the president was met with all the military regalia and American flags the university could muster. Cheerleaders, all male of course, wore white sweaters with big F's. The Commander in Chief's car, carrying Father Gannon and Archbishop Spellman, traveled through the Third Avenue gate as

10,000 people lined the tree-lined pathways to Edward's Parade, stopping at the steps of Keating Hall.

Father Gannon, no Democrat (he described himself as a third generation Republican), made a polite, diplomatic introductory speech that was carefully worded so as to avoid heaping direct praise on the president, but it turned out to be incredibly prescient. As printed in *The Ram* on October 31, 1940, Gannon said:

"It is hard to imagine an occasion of greater interest than a visit from the President of the United States, especially as it is the first time in a hundred years that a President has visited our historic campus. It is true that men destined to the Presidency have been here before. We have a big, friendly boulder out in front, which marks the spot where George Washington slept, perhaps the only such spot in the East — but that was before he took the oath of office.

"The same is true of Mr. Roosevelt. His associations with Fordham go back a number of years; his father's cousin, James Roosevelt Bayley, built old St. John's and the Church nearly a century ago, and last year his charming mother (if Your Excellency will permit me to say so, the most charming of all the Roosevelts) came here in the pouring rain to unveil a tablet erected in honor of Bishop Bayley.

"Mr. Roosevelt himself has been here before in his brilliant days as Governor of the State of New York, when we were proud to make him an honorary member of the university. But that was back in the incredible twenties, before anyone could imagine the tremendous effect he was to have on national and international affairs.

"Today he comes as our chief executive, Commander in Chief of the Army and Navy, chief depository of the great authority which God gave the American people and which in turn the American people have given to the federal government. No wonder, then, that our faculty, students and alumni, regardless of

116

political creed, feel profoundly moved by the honor shown to Fordham in this visit of the President. But I should perhaps point out to the younger men who may not grasp the full significance of this scene, that Mr. Roosevelt is not just another president. In an era of unusually dynamic personalities he is without doubt one of the three or four most dynamic.

"He will be for our great grand-children the symbol of our generation. Other presidents have come and gone and the quiet tide of American life has shown hardly a ripple. How many of you students here could tell me one single event that took place in the time of Chester Arthur?

"Today you stand before a man whose imprint is forever fixed on our national history. Our country has been reshaped in the last eight years and will never again be just what it was before. So that 50 years from now, when you boys totter back to the campus for the Sesquicentennial, you will probably seek out this spot and tell the third generation that here sat Franklin Roosevelt the day he reviewed our troops, and right there sat the beloved

Photo: Fordham Archives

FDR at Fordham – October 28, 1940.

Archbishop of New York, who had come to grace the occasion as a distinguished alumnus and Bishop Castrensis, Chaplain General of the Army and Navy.

"I hope that you will not have to begin your reminiscences by remarking that in the old days — the Jesuits used to be in charge! Mr. President,

117

these troops, which you do us the honor to review, have succeeded to a military tradition which dates back a half a century ago to the days when General Clarence R. Edwards was a member of our staff. In that far off age of innocence there was no thought given to preparedness.

"For aside from a little Indian fighting here and there, a soldier then was as ornamental as a diplomat. Today, however, these boys are proud to think that in the present crisis they are a part of our great national program, and we are proud to claim them as our own. Nowhere in your travels will you see a group whose hearts and minds are more ready for sacrifice, a group more intelligently patriotic. Students of Fordham, it is my honor to present the President of the United States."

Roosevelt, reportedly speaking off the cuff, alluded to the draft, the "preparedness" mentioned by Gannon, and spoke about the importance of service to one's nation, perhaps foretelling the attack on Pearl Harbor that was still more than a year off. Referring to the Fordham cadet corps and its successor, ROTC, he alluded to the 50-year tradition of military training at Fordham.

Here is the full text of his remarks:

"Your Excellency the Archbishop, my friend the Rector, an old alumnus of yours is back for the first time in a great many years, back again, very proud and happy to have the opportunity of reviewing this brigade of which — I should have said battalion, I always get mixed up with military terms as an old Navy man — this battalion of which I have heard so much.

"I should like to come back and see more of the work of the battalion and of the university and I think that the suggestion that the Rector [Gannon] made to my mother would be very welcome on this cold afternoon had I but the time to accept his kind invitation. But I hope that if he should ask me to spend the night he would not ask me to sleep on George Washington's boulder.

So I am glad to be here to see these members of the battalion who know our National Preparedness Program.

"You know that we are to take this muster — and I like to call it muster — because it is an old word that goes back to the old Colonial days in America when every able man had an obligation to serve his community and his country in case of attack. We have mustered a large number of young men. We have done it because, primarily we like to have them trained in the things they will need in the event of an attack, because we feel that in their training we are saving against attack, the lives of all other men in America, the lives of all the women in America, and all the children and therefore this training to make you able to use those new facilities of warfare, to teach you how best to defend America.

"That is our great objective. I am proud of your record of 50 years. I am glad to see you today and I am especially happy to be here on this glorious day in October, this day at the beginning of your Centenary."

That night President Roosevelt spoke to 22,000 people at Madison Square Garden, the first political campaign speech to be televised.

The centenary celebration to which President Roosevelt referred in 1941 was a year-long affair with celebration after celebration. Father Gannon had mounted a Fordham Centenary Appeal for $1,000,000, which started with a bit of a whimper, but raised $600,000, still less than the targeted amount. The less-than-stellar response was explained by former New York State Governor Al Smith who said, "Catholics in this town are not interested in higher education. You have to show them a starving baby."

Gannon also invited a number of prominent guest lecturers to speak: Archduke Otto of Austria, Dr. Hu Shih, the Chinese ambassador, Rear Admiral Richard Byrd, and held numerous symposiums. There was a production of Oedipus Tyrannus by

Sophocles in the original Greek, staged at the newly renovated Collins Auditorium.

The finale of the centennial was a three-day affair from September 15th to the 17th, with representatives of colleges and universities from around the world.

First, a garden party was held with hundreds of guests and a Pontifical Mass. Then the university held a formal dinner at the Waldorf Astoria, where 18 Archbishops and Bishops, and 2200 guests, heard speeches from Vice President Henry A. Wallace and Governor Herbert H. Lehman. Wallace, apropos of the time, spoke about the war in Europe. He defended the policies of President Roosevelt and Winston Churchill by saying they were in keeping with the peace proposals of Pope Pius XII, the previously noted friend of Gannon and Archbishop Spellman.

Finally, there was a convocation on the third day and the campus was decked out with American flags, reminiscent of the 75th anniversary in 1916. Again, thousands gathered on a glorious fall day.

It has been observed that each time Fordham held a jubilee, war was in the air. The silver jubilee came at the end of the Civil War. The Spanish-American War coincided with the golden jubilee. World War I began just prior to the diamond anniversary.

Now, World War II was beckoning Americans to Europe once again and a Fordham celebration was marked by whispering about U.S. involvement overseas. Many students had already enlisted, some 654.

Father Gannon summed it all up when he wrote the following:

"It all seemed such a pity. Just at the time when thoughtful educators were bringing some order into American universities, and even the public was beginning to see the point; when life was returning to the teaching of the liberal arts and an appetite for something beyond facts was developing in American students; when hardheaded employers were beginning to take an interest in

120

the intangibles of a cultured boy – along came a war and shifted all the emphasis back to machines again. Just at a time when Fordham was beginning to see its way clear to the fulfillment of its dreams, a brilliant faculty and a select student body with all the instruments they needed for distinguished service, along came a war and dried up the indispensable sources of help."

Chapter VIII:
Fordham Becomes a World War II Force

On December 7, 1941, the day of the Pearl Harbor bombing by the Japanese, costing 2400 American lives, Fordham lost two alumni, one from the class of 1935 and one from 1937. The announcement about the invasion was actually made during a football game at the Polo Grounds as Fordham was playing NYU. The university would change immensely in the days that followed. By 1944, Father Gannon was lamenting the incredible drop in the student population, due to enlistment and the draft. From an earlier high of more than 9,000, by October of that year, the number had fallen by more than half. Those remaining included a number of women (in the downtown schools), 4Fs (those rejected by the armed forces) and boys under 18. In 1944, Fordham College had just 24 graduates. The undergraduate degree program was amended to allow students to study during the summer and to graduate after three years, a consequence of the war.

Photo: Fordham Archives

The Vincent Building just north of City Hall.

Gannon was swimming upstream, but still trying to make improvements. As stated, he made some adjustments to Collins Auditorium, making it safer in case of fire and adding the theatre-in-the-round to the second floor. Downtown, he secured space at 134 East 39th Street for the School of Social Service. He also purchased the Vincent Building, 302 Broadway, at the corner of Broadway and Duane Street, from the family of William Astor for $122,000, an incredible buy, and placed the Schools of Law, Education and Business there. Then, he established the School of Adult Education, now the School of General Studies. (An uptown Manhattan campus was in the idea stages at this time.)

In 1943, Matthew Ebenezer Adams was the first enrolled Black student at Rose Hill, though it can be claimed that the earliest students of the 1800's from Latin America and South America were not Caucasian. He was pre-med, withdrew to enter the navy in World War II, and returned to graduate in 1947. Two others followed: Harcourt G. Harris, pre-med, and Denis Glennon Baron, an economics major, both from the class of 1948. Baron went on to teach at Fordham and then to work for the State Department in South Asia. Others were already studying at the graduate schools downtown.

This was no small matter since there had been years of debate on the subject of race equality at the Jesuit schools and Fordham had very publicly rejected a Black student named Hudson J. Oliver, Jr., a St. Francis Xavier High School graduate and the son of a distinguished physician in 1934. When, in 1907, a native Japanese student was admitted to the college, much was made of it in the Jesuit publication, the *Woodstock Letters*. In 1904, that same publication reported, "the number of Latin Americans who applied for admission was so large that it was thought unwise to take more than half of them."

The business at hand, of course, was the war. After returning from a trip to London, Gannon was informed that Fordham would be home to two units of the Army Specialized Training Program, subsidized by the government, whose first soldiers arrived in June 1943. Fordham secured eight temporary buildings constructed at a cost of $600,000, only $20,000 of which came out of the university's coffers. The structures were two stories high with wooden exits and entrances that had been declared unfit for human habitation by the military, according to Dr. Andrew B. Myers, class of 1940, who later became an English professor.

"They were placed behind the gymnasium where there then was a lot of grass and open space and given names like Reidy Hall and King-O'Neill – the names of war casualties. The stairs creaked; the floors shook under you. You kept waiting for the moment in which you had to leap out a window in case they burned down," said Dr. Myers.

Soldiers were put everywhere, even the gym, causing its wooden floor to sink and changing the nature of basketball games for a time thereafter.

More than 4,730 students from Fordham would serve in many capacities. One Fordham man, John W. Clauss (1919-2013), class of 1941, was a U.S. Army Air Force meteorologist advising General Eisenhower, Supreme Allied Commander, on whether the weather was right for the Normandy Invasion. The attack was originally planned for June 5th, but had to be postponed a day due to storms, possibly predicted by Clauss.

Two hundred twenty-nine Fordham men gave their lives, 29 at the Battle of the Bulge.

With surprising forethought, the government was already making plans for the post-war years and what it believed would be a boom at colleges. The GI Bill, officially the Serviceman's Readjustment Act, was passed in 1944 to subsidize college for veterans and would open the floodgates.

At Fordham, there would soon be an influx of students. As Father Gannon negotiated with government officials about how many students Fordham could handle, he made some changes to the curriculum and to the overall university marketing strategy.

The priest who hired a public relations firm decided Fordham needed a more robust communications program, first known as the Department of Communication Arts, to include the study of journalism (moved from the English department), radio and later

124

television and film. It also encompassed theater at first, including the performances of the Mimes and Mummers theatre troupe. Established in 1946, there was funding from the family of Joseph Medill Patterson, founder of the *New York Daily News*, for a Patterson Chair of Journalism (first held by Professor David Marshall) and a number of Patterson scholarships. The first department chairman was Professor Ed Walsh who had a long career at Fordham that left a lasting impression on many students and faculty members from the communications department. He held the Patterson Chair for many years. Creative writing was part of the first course catalogue as taught by Rev. Alfred Barrett, S.J., a published poet who was described as "rakish" and "used the old Jesuit cape to great dramatic effect," according to Professor Jack Phelan, later head of the department.

Gannon also decided to spend $49,600 of money donated by the Michael P. Grace II Fund to establish Fordham University's Voice, the 50,000-watt radio station, WFUV in 1947. The dedication, with Cardinal Spellman presiding, was held on October 26th. The station would broadcast at 90.7 FM, as it does today. At the time it could be heard up to 40 miles away. The reach is much wider now due to a new antenna and new transmitter technology. Originally, and for many years thereafter, the station was run by students and broadcast "eclectic" programming. There was classical music, news, round-table discussions and even full-length theater productions.

Today the station, an affiliate of National Public Radio and no longer run by the students, serves approximately 350,000 listeners weekly in the New York metropolitan area. The format is called "adult alternative" and is still a mix of different kinds of talk and music on the weekends. In 2012, the *Princeton Review* ranked WFUV as the 10th most popular college radio station in the U.S. In the 1960's, Father Gannon bragged that the communications program at Fordham had produced a Vatican correspondent for the *Associated Press*, an editor for *The New York Times* and numerous vice presidents of radio and television networks, not to mention the many who went on to own advertising and public relations firms. Today, some of the names of these graduates are well known to audiences throughout the country – Charles Osgood (originally Charles Woods, but there was already at Charles Woods at *CBS* where he would work for the next 50+ years), Vince Scully (LA Dodgers broadcaster), Michael Kay (voice of the New York Yankees) and countless others in jobs in or related to broadcasting.

Fordham may have been a bit of a ghost town during the war, saved for the troops stationed there, but afterwards all of the extra buildings would be needed for the thousands who returned from service overseas seeking an education.

That fact was confirmed by Frank G. M. Corbin, class of 1950, a communication arts major who had a long career in media and public relations and stayed close to Fordham as an adjunct professor of advertising and PR from 1953 until 2012. Corbin had been drafted directly out of high school in 1943 and went straight into the Army, serving beyond the war's end. Following service in the 26th Infantry in northern France, Corbin was made a second lieutenant and sent to Germany to act as a liaison between Washington's elite and those in charge at the Nuremberg trials. He remembered hearing the testimony of Hermann Goring, whom he described as having the highest IQ of all the prisoners by far. He listened to the testimony of Rudolf Hess, Julius Streicher and others.

According to Corbin, World War II was a significant factor in changing the complexion at many, particularly Catholic colleges, whose fates were saved by the fact that the Army and Navy placed training programs on campus.

Corbin recalled the huge influx of students when he arrived in 1946. "For the college at Rose Hill," he said, "we needed a second section that started in 1946-47. There was a day shift of classes and then a night shift. Some faculty members were working from nine in the morning until nine at night."

It became so chaotic at times that the university established the *Fordham Flash*. Likely an homage to the famous baseball player of the post-World War I years, the *Flash* was a bulletin issued every morning that alerted students and teachers to daily changes. Classes were moved from one classroom to another, if more students were added. Teachers were redeployed. Students were even advised through this vehicle about where they should register to get their checks from the Veteran's Administration. The *Flash* lasted five years.

From 1944 to 1949, registration was up to an all-time high of 13,200, according to Father Gannon. This didn't make him happy given his previous efforts to keep enrollment down to an elite few. He reported that Governor Thomas Dewey and the state commissioner of education would call him frequently asking him to take another 300 or so students. Their pleas were frequently accompanied by promises to fund more temporary buildings.

In 1947 alone, 800 freshmen were accepted to Fordham, about 350 more than the faculty thought it could handle properly. Students came from other states and even other countries and there was a need for housing, hence the building of Cardinal Spellman Hall behind Keating, named for Father Gannon's friend and benefactor. Spellman Hall was later used to house Jesuit priests and scholastics, and in 1967, became the first women's residence hall.

Said Corbin, "People who never dreamed of higher education, found themselves in college. I had classmates from age 17 to 37. (The youngest was the actor Pat Harrington, Jr. who went on to star in the TV sitcom, "One Day at a Time.") Some were married with kids. This gave a totally different picture to the campus and made it different for the faculty. The old, 'yes, father, no father' attitude of prior students was a thing of the past. Teachers were no longer able to use the patent formula of instructing because students were now unafraid to challenge them. They had been to war, for Pete's sake."

Corbin said Father Gannon complained publicly and bitterly that the GI Bill brought evil, though the president played that down later on. According to Corbin, Gannon snidely called President Truman "the man hand-picked by the late President Roosevelt to succeed him." Gannon thought the GI Bill placed people in college who should not have been there, which led to turmoil and overcrowding. He was part of the old guard, convinced that higher education was for the privileged.

Corbin, his classmates, and even professors, vehemently disagreed and believed the veterans were a boon to the university, increasing not only its size, but also the level of dialogue between students and professors.

"The veterans were looking for an education and a degree," said Corbin. "They were more mature and took a different view of everything on campus. They valued education and what it would mean to them and to their families. These students were more serious, really, than the kids who arrived from high school for a good time because their parents decided to send them off to college."

Rev. William Reilly, S.J., a philosophy professor said, "My first class was two-thirds veterans; they were a fine group to teach."

Denis McInerney, class of 1948, whose studies were interrupted during the war chimed in, saying, "When I arrived at Rose Hill, I was still in my paratroop uniform and wearing my boots. That went on for the first few weeks because there was a real shortage of men's civilian clothing. The war had ended sooner than expected due to the atomic bomb, and no one had any inventory. It was very difficult to get good threads, as they say today. Having come back from a pretty bombed-out Europe, the campus looked great to me. Everyone was quite friendly, either because they had shared the same experience, or because they were interested in what happened. It was very easy to locate a group in the cafeteria that would be a congenial group."

The post-war years delivered a number of interesting personalities to Fordham, many of whom would never have been there otherwise. Louis Budenz, a Soviet spy and former editor of the Communist newspaper, the *Daily Worker*, taught economics. Budenz, who later renounced communism and returned to the Catholic Church, had been a major leader of the Communist party in the U.S. According to Corbin, "He was an amazing teacher. He would walk into the classroom and start talking and wouldn't stop until the 50 minutes was over. He would neither ask nor entertain questions, which was different. He was incredibly intelligent and knowledgeable, but my impression was that he didn't want to have personal contact with anyone."

More interesting, perhaps, is that the FBI detailed agents to the Rose Hill campus to keep an eye on Budenz. "They were supposed to look like students and fit in," said Corbin, "but J. Edgar Hoover had ordered everyone in the FBI to wear hats, so we always knew who they were. Most students didn't come to class in the typical G-Man outfit."

Another well-known professor in the communication arts department was the only child of one of the most famous actresses of the 40's and 50's, Marlene Dietrich. Her name was Maria Elizabeth Sieber, later known as Maria Riva. It was legend for years that Ms. Riva married her husband, William Riva, a theatre arts professor and set designer, at the University Church with Ms. Dietrich in attendance. While the couple did meet at Fordham, Ms. Riva told me the wedding story was apocryphal like so many other stories about celebrities, and that her mother wasn't even in the country when the actual ceremony took place at the Cathedral of St. John the Divine in July 1948. "Read my book," she said, referring to her 1993 tome, *Marlene Dietrich*, largely about her relationship with her mother.

Still, Maria Riva and her husband loved Fordham, even years after they moved on to long and successful careers on stage and television. Riva said she adored the people, the creativity and even the freedom of expression. There were few theatrical restrictions imposed by the Jesuits, she said, except that the works of certain playwrights like Tennessee Williams and George Bernard Shaw were not to be produced in Collins Auditorium.

At Fordham just after the end of the war, Riva said there was a euphoric feeling about the U.S. and its role in winning the conflict overseas. For her, the optimism she felt was a welcome change after her time spent as a USO performer in Europe, where the American troops had been understandably on edge.

"The feeling at Rose Hill was great," she said. "I loved working there. It was free-thinking and wonderful. You never had the feeling that it was conservative."

She remembered that the Jesuits always tipped their hats to the ladies, except Father Gannon who only did so, she said, when she was noticeably pregnant with her first child. Another memory was of having White Castle hamburgers delivered to the Collins theatre during rehearsals.

Of the four sons of Maria and William Riva, one, Paul, attended Fordham.

Even the prized boxer Rocky Marciano, Heavy Weight Champion of the World 1952-56, was rumored to have spent time at Fordham during these years, though neither as a student nor a teacher. After visiting the campus for a "Night of Sports," Marciano, who said he needed R & R and a break from some personal issues, holed up in the gym and ended up staying four or five days incognito. Said Frank Corbin, "there were so many people on campus that no would one have ever bothered to check on anyone or to notice one more person." Marciano ate and slept with the students until he decided he was ready to go back home.

In 1946, Gannon, ever the PR man, reflected that the centenary celebration held in 1941 had been scaled down because of the impending war and cooked up another to commemorate the 100th anniversary of the university's charter in 1846.

In spite of his differences with Democratic politicians, Gannon had up his sleeve the visit of another Democratic U.S. President, Harry S. Truman, on whom he planned to confer an honorary Doctor of Laws alongside Governor Thomas E. Dewey, a Republican. In an ironic twist, perhaps foretelling of the next presidential election in 1948, Dewey had to be told by a sheepish Gannon that the White House had stipulated that when the President of the United States receives an honorary degree, he is the only one to do so. Dewey's response, according to Gannon: "Protocol? Hell! It's politics!" Dewey was right. When there was a request to present a degree to England's Archbishop of Westminster on the same day, the White House gave its blessing.

Truman's visit, May 11th, meant a new name for the Terrace of the Presidents and brought 6,000 people to the campus. In addition to his nationally broadcast (on radio) speech, Truman was the first to ring Fordham's historic Victory Bell. The bell was a gift to the university from Fleet

Photo: Fordham Archives
President Harry Truman and Admiral Chester Nimitz.

131

Admiral Chester W. Nimitz of the U.S. Navy, and a Fordham
Law graduate, "as a Memorial to Our Dear Young Dead of
World War II." From the Japanese aircraft carrier Junyo,
destroyed by torpedoes at Saipan during the war, the bell still
hangs in front of the Rose Hill gym and is supposed to be rung
following all Ram athletic victories and at the start of
commencement each year.

Truman, who did not go to college, but served in France as a
captain in the army during World War I, defended the GI Bill in
his remarks delivered at 5 p.m. from Keating Terrace:

"Your Eminences, President Gannon, fellow alumni and
friends, it is very gratifying to be here at Fordham University in
New York on the One Hundredth Anniversary of the granting of
the charter to this great institution of higher learning. I am very
grateful for this degree of Doctor of Laws from Fordham. I am
happy to become a fellow alumnus of the men who have gone
out from Fordham and who are making such a substantial
contribution to the government and to their communities.

"One of my able Secretaries is a graduate of this great
institution, Mr. Matthew Connelly.

"I should like in these few minutes to talk especially of the
veterans who have enrolled in this university. For I think that
there is great significance in the very fact of their being here - and
of the veterans being in thousands of other universities, colleges,
and schools throughout the land.

"This nation has a comprehensive program to return its
veterans to civil life. That program is being carried out. The
federal government, with the wholehearted cooperation of the
various states, has provided many things for veterans -medical
care, rehabilitation, loans for homes and farms and businesses; it
is providing life insurance and soon it will provide adequate
housing. All these benefits are given not as a matter of favor but
as a matter of right. Veterans must not be penalized for their war
service.

"Programs of this nature, though less comprehensive, were established for veterans of past wars. But today we find the beginning of a new and important concept - one which is given concrete evidence by the presence of veterans here today. That concept is that the nation must provide for its veterans something more than pensions, something more than insurance, loans, and rehabilitation. For those who wish it, the nation must also provide education.

"An enormous and tragic deficit was accumulated during the war - a deficit in education-as millions of young men and women left behind them their books and their schools and colleges to go to war. Not only gratitude, but national self-preservation as well, required that this educational deficit be diminished or wiped out. By providing educational benefits for our veterans, the Congress has started us on the way to our goal.

Photo: Fordham Archives
Harry Truman on the Terrace of the Presidents.

"Some doubt was expressed a few years ago as to whether there would be any interest among the veterans in these educational aids. There were those - I call them skeptics or men without faith in the youth of our Nation-who thought that only a handful of veterans would choose to come back to the quiet halls of learning. These men were wrong. The problem is not in the lack of veterans seeking education. The problem is to provide accommodations for those who seek it.

133

Even some colleges, which had been exclusively for women, have had to open their doors to men students. The response of the colleges and schools to this thirst for knowledge of our veterans has been magnificent.

"This desire for further schooling which has been evidenced by our veterans - men and women who will be our leaders of tomorrow – is full of healthy promise for the future.

"And may God give us those leaders, so that we may continue to assume that leadership which God has always intended us to take in this world.

"The fact that so many veterans have taken advantage of these educational opportunities increases the heavy responsibility which rests upon our schools and colleges. In preparing our veterans and other young men and women to live in the new atomic age, education faces the greatest challenge in history.

"There is profound truth in the first line of the new charter of the United Nations Educational, Scientific and Cultural Organization. The charter declares: 'Since wars begin in the minds of men, it is in the minds of men that the defenses of peace must be constructed.'

"I fear we are too much concerned with material things to remember that our real strength lies in spiritual values. I doubt whether there is in this troubled world today, when nations are divided by jealousy and suspicion, a single problem that could not be solved if approached in the spirit of the Sermon on the Mount.

"The new age of atomic energy presses upon us. Mark that well! What may have been sufficient yesterday is not sufficient today. New and terrible urgencies, new and terrible responsibilities, have been placed upon education.

"Ignorance and its handmaidens, prejudice, intolerance, suspicion of our fellow men, breed dictators. And they breed wars. Civilization cannot survive an atomic war. Nothing would be left but a world reduced to rubble. Gone would be man's hope for decency. Gone would be our hope for the greatest age in the history of mankind - an age which I know can harness atomic energy for the welfare of man and not for his destruction.

"And so we must look to education in the long run to wipe out that ignorance which threatens catastrophe. Intelligent men do not hate other men just because their religion may be different, or because their habits and language may be different, or because their national origin or color may be different. It is up to education to bring about that deeper international understanding which is so vital to world peace.

"Intelligent Americans no longer think that merely because a man is born outside the boundaries of the United States, he is no concern of ours. They know that in such thinking lie the seeds of dictatorship and tyranny. And they know from sad experience that dictatorship and tyranny are too ruthless to stop at the borders of the United States and conveniently leave us alone. They know what World War II and the atomic bomb have taught them - that we must work and live with all our fellow men if we are to work and live at all. They know that those without economic hope, those to whom education has been forcibly denied, willingly turn to dictators. They know that in a nation where teachers are free to teach, and young men and women are free to learn, there is a strong bulwark against dictatorship.

"That was the last message from President Roosevelt. In a speech which he wrote just before he died, but which he never delivered, he said:

"'We are faced with the preeminent fact that, if civilization is to survive, we must cultivate the science of human relationships- the ability of all peoples, of all kinds, to live and work together, in the same world, at peace.'

"Until citizens of America, and citizens of the other nations of the world learn this 'science of human relationships' of which President Roosevelt spoke, the atomic bomb will remain a frightful weapon which threatens to destroy all of us.

135

"But there is at least one defense against that bomb. That defense lies in our mastering this science of human relationships all over the world. It is the defense of tolerance and of understanding, of intelligence and thoughtfulness.

"When we have learned these things, we shall be able to prove that Hiroshima was not the end of civilization, but the beginning of a new and better world.

"That is the task which confronts education. The veterans who attend the colleges and schools of today, and the children of the veterans who will go to school tomorrow, have a right to expect that the training offered to them will fulfill that task. It is not an easy task. It is a most difficult one. It is one which places burdens without precedent, both upon those who teach and upon those who come to be taught. There must be new inspiration, new meaning, new energies. There must be a rebirth of education if this new and urgent task is to be met.

"I know that education will meet that challenge. If our civilization is to survive, it must meet it. All of our educational resources must be pledged to that end. The road is hard, but the reward is great.

"I am confident that this splendid institution, with its educational system rounded upon Christian principles, will play a full and noble part in the great adventure ahead of us. We can and we must make the atomic age an age of peace for the glory of God and the welfare of mankind."

As his long and triumphant, but somewhat controversial, presidency neared its end, Gannon had to contend with the failures of the once heralded Fordham football team. The war had cost the university many team members who fled to enlist, including even the coach, Jim Crowley, who became a lieutenant commander in the Navy. There was also now serious enforcement of the NCAA rule that only bona fide students play on teams. Father Gannon, who took the NCAA rules to heart and believed in them, caught a great deal of flak from the alumni and the vociferous sports reporters of the time.

He didn't seem to care. During a speech to the alumni that was supposed to be "off-the-record," the university president angered the sports community in New York by saying, "We are not interested in providing business for the gambling fraternity. We are not interested in catering to the subway circuit as a whole. We are interested in staging contests for our students, the alumni, friends and those in the subway that cross themselves." He referred to the managers of Randall's Island where Fordham played football as "extortionists" and the sportswriters of the day as the "tyrants of tyrants." (Interestingly, while he alludes to this incident in his own book about Fordham, Gannon does not provide his exact words – though the newspapers of the time did, including *The New York Times* on October 20, 1947.) The football program continued to lose money and even a short stint by Vince Lombardi as assistant coach in 1947 didn't help.

One of Father Gannon's last acts as president was to raise $1.2 million from a benefactor, the largest university gift to date, to build a new dorm in the style of Queens Court, the immense building that would be known as Martyr's Court. It commemorates three French Jesuits slain by the Iroquois on the Mohawk River in the 1640's, Isaac Jogues, Rene Goupil and Jean Lalande.

Chapter IX:
The Cold War

From 1949 to 1963, Laurence J. McGinley was president of Fordham. Installed on February 2, 1949, his tenure would exceed that of his predecessor in length, giving him the record by one year. Like Gannon, McGinley was able to make a number of changes and advancements, perhaps because he was also given the gift of time. McGinley was more popular among the masses than Gannon. His politics, though conservative, were more mainstream and he was not as strident in his delivery. He was decidedly more humble.

Unfortunately, one of the new president's first challenges turned out to be a huge negative that dominated the final part of Gannon's reign, the demise of the football team, which many attribute to the latter's lack of support.

McGinley ended a 63-year tradition during which Fordham had 254 victories, 159 losses and 35 ties. The team had played in two bowl games, the Cotton Bowl in 1941 (Fordham lost to Texas A&M 13-12) and the Sugar Bowl in 1942 (Fordham beat Missouri, 2-0). The overriding opinion was that the university administration was not behind the program, though it claimed otherwise. In addition, the program continued to carry financial losses.

It was said that too few people were packing the stands because the team was then playing on Randall's Island, an inconvenient location reachable only by car or bus. Also, the student body, then made up of older students with families and jobs, did not have time to attend football games. Even the alumni stopped showing up. Pro football was catching on in popularity during these years, another reason for the lack of support.

A more specific problem was the fact that the team captain, Jack Hyatt, 1951's most valuable player, was stricken with polio. He eventually recovered, but was no longer able to play football.

When *The Ram* ran an editorial criticizing the university's handling of the whole football matter, the editor was relieved of his duties.

Then two poor seasons befell the team, in 1953 and 1954, and it was all over. Father McGinley made the decision that the university could no longer support the losses, emotionally and financially, and put an end to Fordham and football. The statement he issued to the public said, "at long last, our head must rule our heart."

Despite the unpopularity of that decision early in his term, McGinley, with a paternalistic demeanor, was the right man at the right time for the job. He emphasized the *cura personalis*, the Jesuit responsibility for personal care that characterized the Fordham education and remains its base today, often mentioned by later President Joseph McShane. He was known to address his audiences as members of the "Fordham family," a phrase adopted by a number of his successors. A New Yorker who graduated from St. Francis Xavier High School in 1922, McGinley had an oratorical gift and patrician attitude made possible by a deep baritone voice, honed during a stint working for Vatican Radio in the late 1930's – and as a teacher.

McGinley was dedicated to students as individuals and was committed to the teaching of values that he believed were dwindling during the 50's and 60's. Part of his challenge was the growth of higher education in general and specific changes in the Fordham curriculum made inevitable by evolution at other U.S. colleges and universities. There would be still fewer classes taught in the tradition of the Jesuit education and more and more emphasis on the sciences, and that bane of the Jesuits – practica institutione (practical education). It's doubtful that the likes of Father Thébaud and Father Tellier from the 19th century would

139

have condoned the teaching of computer science or radio news writing.

In these days, Fordham students still had curfews. Rev. J. Quentin Lauer, S.J., a professor of philosophy, lived among the students in Martyr's Court for 35 years. Years later, he said, "It was expected, demanded really, that all students be in by 11:00 at night, at least on weekdays, and every one of them on my floor had to come in and report to me. Then I had to check off that they had come in to see me. Obnoxious in some ways, but in another way, I look back and wish we had something like it still. Every single night I saw every single student, and I got to know them, which is not true today."

Classes still began with a prayer. Dr. Norman O. Smith, not a Catholic, remembered being asked to open classes with either three Hail Mary's or one Lord's Prayer. "Being an Episcopalian, I chose the Lord's Prayer," he said. He also remembered being in the cafeteria, then in the basement of Keating Hall, and asking for a ham sandwich on a Friday. That, said the person next to him on line, was frowned upon.

It wasn't the 60's yet, but the decade of Eisenhower, generally considered one of peace and tranquility on the homeland, brought the introduction of interracial issues and activities with the Campus Interracial Council, begun by Rev. William Reilly, S.J., and an Interracial Sunday once a month. Father Reilly, who said he welcomed the civil rights movement and the stress on affirmative action, said "we would have a special mass, a special preacher, as we called them in those days, and our Father [John] LaFarge was here with us. So we were taking steps then which were part of the development, and, as we look back, too slow development, of involving the minority students." LaFarge, the son of the painter and stained glass artist who had graduated from Fordham, wrote several pre-World War II articles decrying racism, one of which caught the attention of Pope Pius XI, who asked him to prepare a papal pronouncement against racist and totalitarian ideologies.

Though the rigorous curriculums of the past were gone, intellectual advancement continued. McGinley, with help from the Dean of Fordham College, Thurston Davis, was finally able to get Phi Beta Kappa to establish a chapter at Fordham in 1958. There was also the development of the Golden Alpha, an honors society for those whose grade point average never slipped below 3.5. Such graduates received their degrees "summa cum laude in cursu honorum," the latter of which translates to "in a course of honors." Today, students receiving the degree are distinguished as honor students with 3.5 GPAs by the end of senior year.

Rev. Joseph Frese, S.J., professor of history in the 50's, later academic vice president and acting president for a time, ran the honors program in the 50's and remembered it fondly. Students and teachers would gather for dinner before the evening seminars at a little Italian restaurant just under the Third Avenue El. He recalled being served three- and four-course dinners for $1.25.

Photo: Fordham Archives

Alan Alda gave the commencement address in 1978.

For teachers who were not performing well, even Jesuits, there was trouble and some were dismissed. Davis founded the Institute of Contemporary Russian Studies in the summer of 1950, perhaps a foretelling of the Cold War. He also started a study abroad program for juniors that would take them to Paris for the school year.

One student who took advantage of the chance to go to Europe was a member of the class of 1956. Born Alphonso Joseph D'Abruzzo, he is better known to most of us as Alan

Alda, the Oscar and Emmy award-winning actor who portrayed the iconic Hawkeye Pierce for 11 years on M*A*S*H – the TV sitcom set at an American army hospital during the Korean War. (Alda was a combination of the first two letters of his first and last names.) He later became known as a writer, movie actor and producer. Alda, the son of then-famous actor and singer Robert Alda (Broadway's Guys and Dolls), was a member of the Fordham theatre troupe, Mimes and Mummers, and worked at WFUV. Spending his junior year abroad allowed him to act in a play in Rome and to perform with his father on television in Amsterdam. At Fordham, he was also a member of ROTC. After receiving his degree in English, he served out his ROTC time for a year at Fort Benning, Georgia. He then joined the U.S. Army Reserves for six months as a gunnery officer.

Not coincidentally, the M*A*S*H character, Dr. Pierce, was written as a Fordham graduate, a fact mentioned in many scripts since Alda wrote 19 episodes. The actor has returned to Fordham on many occasions, most notably as commencement speaker in 1978. Since M*A*S*H, Alda has starred in dozens of movies, a number of Broadway plays and still more television programs. He has also been a champion of human rights and environmental causes. The Jesuits of the 1950's Fordham might not have been happy to hear that in his book, *Things I Overheard While Talking to Myself*, Alda spoke of leaving his Roman Catholic roots behind:

"For a while in my teens, I was sure I had it. It was about getting to heaven. If heaven existed and lasted forever, then a mere lifetime spent scrupulously following orders was a small investment for an infinite payoff. One day, though, I realized I was no longer a believer, and realizing that, I couldn't go back. Not that I lost the urge to pray. Occasionally, even after I stopped believing, I might send off a quick memo to the Master of the Universe, usually on a matter needing urgent attention, like Oh, God, don't let us crash. These were automatic expulsions of

142

words, brief SOS messages from the base of my brain. They were similar to the short prayers that were admired by the church in my Catholic boyhood, which they called 'ejaculations.' I always liked the idea that you could shorten your time in purgatory with each ejaculation; what boy wouldn't find that a comforting idea? But my effort to keep the plane in the air by talking to God didn't mean I suddenly was overcome with belief, only that I was scared. Whether I'd wake up in heaven someday or not, whatever meaning I found would have to occur first on this end of eternity."

Speaking further on agnosticism, Alda said:

"I still don't like the word agnostic. It's too fancy. I'm simply not a believer. But, as simple as this notion is, it confuses some people. Someone wrote a *Wikipedia* entry about me, identifying me as an atheist because I'd said in a book I wrote that I wasn't a believer. I guess in a world uncomfortable with uncertainty, an unbeliever must be an atheist, and possibly an infidel. This gets us back to that most pressing of human questions: why do people worry so much about other people's holding beliefs other than their own?"

Best-selling author Don DeLillo did not have a famous father, but he entered Fordham at about the same time as Alda and also went on to respectable fame in the arts as a novelist. He graduated with the class of 1958 having majored in communication arts. From the Belmont neighborhood in the Bronx and a graduate of Cardinal Hayes High School, DeLillo remembered Fordham in the 1950's *somewhat* fondly. He told *The New York Times* in 1982 that he hated school, but "the Jesuits taught me to be a failed ascetic."

Father Schroth writes that Fordham became a somewhat social place during the 1950's and featured the big-time orchestras of the time, like Lester Lanin. He reports, "in one beautifully chaotic moment at a freshman dance in April 1953, a big car pulled up in front of the gym late at night. The doors flew open and Jimmy Durante, followed by his entourage of singer-dancer Eddie Jackson, drummer Jules Buffano and other hangers-on, burst out of the car like 20 circus clowns pouring out of a Volkswagen. They swept up the steps, through the doors and onto the bandstand. Durante took over the piano, threw the sheet music into the air, heaved the piano top to Buffano and played and sang [his trademark] 'Inka Dinka Doo.' Eddie Jackson, strutting his top hat and tux, sang 'Bill Bailey, Won't You Please Come Home.' Then, pandemonium having been established, they were gone."

During this decade, McGinley was able to reorganize the upper echelon of the university administration by naming four officers who answered directly to the president: the academic vice-president, the vice-president for business and finance, the director of student personnel and the director of university development, which eventually morphed into vice presidencies. Later a director of research and program development was named along with an executive vice-president and an academic vice president, previously the provost.

He reestablished the public relations program begun under Gannon, but abandoned during the war, and set out to get positive publicity in the media for the university and to raise funds. This brought more than $3 million to Fordham, some from an Alumni Annual Giving Program. In 1952, the number of alumni was said to be 30,000. By 1966, Fordham was 33rd on a list of 37 private universities having an endowment of more than $5 million. At $8.5 million, it was sixth among Catholic colleges.

Father McGinley was likewise able to take advantage of government subsidies and the emergence of philanthropic foundations willing to support institutions of higher learning, all of which were emerging at this time. But, he also had to contend with students going off to fight yet another war, this time the conflict in Korea.

In 1950, *The Ram* wrote in an editorial:

144

"Several students have already left Rose Hill as a result of the aggression in Korea. More will, undoubtedly follow. Young men will have to be ready to march as long as an Iron Curtain darkens one half of the world and threatens twilight at several points in the other section."

Two hundred sixteen students from Fordham fought and three died – Richard Prohl and Joseph J. Kiernan, both of the class of 1951, and U.S. Navy Lieutenant James Noble, class of 1947, who had been a star football player prior to World War II. He had returned to Fordham as a student and assistant coach.

As the U.S. was fighting the North Koreans and the Cold War was evolving, the newly implemented Russian studies program caused a stir. Introduced by Father Thurston Davis, dean of Fordham College, it was set up to answer the need for more knowledge about the newly imposing Soviet Union. Partially funded by an appropriation from the National Defense Education Act, the curriculum became well known and was even lampooned by the Russians.

According to Rev. Walter Jaskievicz, S.J., director of the Institute of Contemporary Russian Studies from 1952 to 1969, the program involved conducting research with the Army Map Service and the CIA, and ultimately stood accused of subversive activities. He attributed that to the fact that the CIA was in disfavor at that time.

Years after the program was phased out and integrated into the modern languages department, Father Jaskievicz said, "I regret that we missed the opportunity of developing the institute into a real ideological center of research on the influence and spread of atheism in the Soviet Union and the world at large. We predicted the weakening of Soviet and Marxist ideology in 75 years; it is happening. We needed a bit more publicity of the right kind."

Amusingly, publicity came from the Soviet magazine, *Ogonyok*, which ran a cartoon alluding to Fordham's "spy school." Said Father Jaskievicz, "It pictured the typical professor in cap and gown instructing the typical student, who was unshaven with close cropped hair and with a cigarette dangling from the side of his mouth. Grenades, pistols and knives protruded from various parts of his clothing as he watched the professor trace the trajectory of a bomb falling on a factory. A cute verse mentioned that Fordham had inaugurated a spy school in 1950 and it was not flourishing."

A 1952 Fordham graduate who served in the army during Korea and the Cold War, who would probably have been in favor of the Russian studies program, was Watergate figure G. Gordon Liddy. Contrary to conventional wisdom that Liddy had earned some of his eccentricities while serving in the war, he actually remained stateside during his Army service as an artillery officer because he had an enlarged heart. Later he attended Fordham Law School and held a position on the *Fordham Law Review*. After that, he signed on with the FBI to serve under J. Edgar Hoover where, according to *Nixonland: The Rise of a President and the Fracturing of America* by Rick Perlstein, he was referred to by a supervisor as "a wild man" and a "superklutz."

At Fordham as an undergrad, Liddy was a legacy student who had grown up in Hoboken. His father, Sylvester, had been a track star and president of the drama club in the 1920's. The son joined the Republican Club and ran successfully for student government and boarder council. He also worked at WFUV. He wrote in his autobiography, *Will*, that when he was young he tested his own strength and endurance by eating rats and subjecting himself to pain. He also alluded to sympathy for the Nazis, influenced by a German maid/nanny from his childhood. Liddy's autobiography also claims that the Nazi SS troops had looked to the Jesuits as a model of discipline.

Liddy and E. Howard Hunt organized and directed the Watergate burglaries of the Democratic National Committee headquarters at the Watergate complex in 1972. Five of Liddy's operatives were arrested inside the DNC offices on June 17 of that year. Subsequent investigation, thanks to the *Washington Post's* Carl Bernstein and Bob Woodward, led to President Nixon's resignation in 1974. Liddy was convicted of burglary, conspiracy and refusing to testify before the Senate committee investigating Watergate. He served nearly 52 months in federal prison. His career was revived after prison as a radio talk show host and lecturer. He has visited Fordham to speak at least three

Photo: Fordham Archives
Father McGinley with Senator Jack Kennedy.

times and has often credited the Jesuits for teaching him "how to think, not what to think." Liddy's three sons attended Fordham in the 1980's.

As the 1960 presidential election neared, the two main candidates, Liddy's future boss, then-Vice President Richard Nixon, and Massachusetts Senator John F. Kennedy, were invited to speak as part of the Student Government's American Age lecture series. The vice president made it on Wednesday, October 5th. Senator Kennedy did not, though he did make a speech at the corner of Fordham Road and the Grand Concourse on November 5, 1960, just days before the election. The future president had received an honorary degree at the Fordham Law Association luncheon on February 15, 1958, saying, "As your newest alumnus, I wish to deny emphatically that I have any presidential aspirations—with respect to the Fordham Alumni Association."

Among the guests in the gym to hear Nixon that day was New York State's Lieutenant Governor (and later Governor) Malcolm Wilson, a Republican of Fordham class of 1933 (a prep and law

147

graduate as well), for whom the Tappan Zee Bridge is officially named. The partial text of Nixon's remarks, incredibly telling of events to come in the U.S., is as follows:

"Governor [Nelson] Rockefeller, my fellow vice president, president of the student body, all of the distinguished guests, Lieutenant Governor Wilson, and friends of Fordham, I am certainly very honored that I have been given the opportunity to address this convocation of Fordham students and friends of this great institution.

"There are many reasons why I feel that way. The first, of course, is the obvious one to which Father [Victor] Yanitelli [VP for Student Affairs] referred – that I happen to be one of those who have received an honorary degree [1959] from this institution, and I'm glad to be at least an honorary alumnus. I don't think that I could pass the course today, but I'm glad to get it free.

Photo: Fordham Archives

Vice President Nixon posed with a live Fordham Ram. Notice the campaign button on the mascot's forehead.

"It really wasn't entirely free. I had to make a speech. But, be that as it may, I also want to say that I was very pleased to hear the Fordham band playing "California, Here I Come." Going back a few years, to the days of Rose Hill to Rose Bowl, I would think that's what they were referring to, but I know that it referred to me on this occasion, and we certainly appreciate that.

"I know, of course, there are not many among those in the student body these days who remember the great series between

148

Fordham and St. Mary's, and remember that year when those great Fordham football teams should have been invited to the Rose Bowl, but some way or another we Westerners made a mistake and invited somebody we could beat for a change. We haven't done it for a while, but...

"Today I do not want to talk to you in terms solely of the political debate that's going on in the country. You will have plenty of opportunity to see that and to hear it, and I imagine to participate in it.

"I want to talk to you about the great issue of our time, and I do not want to miss the opportunity to talk particularly to those of you who are students here about the contributions you can make and, as a matter of fact you must make, to the solution of those issues.

"And, so, I begin with the greatest issue, already implied by the introduction, and that is, of course, the issue of survival, one that has been brought to our attention, as Father McGinley was indicating when I called upon him a few moments ago, by the presence of Mr. [Nikita] Khrushchev [then Soviet leader] in the United States.

"We see this man. We see in his face, in his actions, in his unpredictability, in his ruthlessness - we see the challenge that America and the free world faces today.

"There is no disagreement among us as to whether we ought to meet this challenge. Whether we are Democrats or Republicans or Independents we all believe that it is essential to develop a program which will win the peace, win the peace without losing our freedom, and that will extend freedom throughout the world.

"And I think this we should all understand at the beginning. As a matter of fact, I would only make one correction to the very eloquent introduction by the president of the student body. He said there were all shades of political coloration here. I would say, except red, in this audience today.

"And that is true of all American audiences throughout the country. Our concern is the same: How do we keep our freedom? How do we extend it? How do we maintain the peace of the world?

"Turning to this point, and looking first at the challenge, there are some obvious conclusions on which we would all agree. First, knowing the man who is the symbol of the opposition to peace and freedom, the one who challenges it, knowing the man, we can reach only one conclusion as to what kind of policies are effective in dealing with him. What does he want? He wants to conquer the world. What means will he use to do it? Any means.

"He would prefer to do it without war, as he said over and over again, although his Chinese colleague, Mao Tse-tung, says that he, as far as he is concerned, would use war, because he, Mao Tse-tung, points to the fact that after the First World War came the Soviet Union, after the Second World War came the expansion of communism to many more countries and approximately a billion people in the world, and after the third world war the whole world will be Communist. This is Mao Tse-tung's reasoning, reasoning which Khrushchev at the moment apparently - and we hopefully say - is not following.

"But, nevertheless, make no mistake; whether he says peaceful co-existence, peaceful competition, whatever he says, he is determined to conquer the world. He believes that communism should rule the world. This we know and, therefore, the line of American policy, of free world policy, is very clear. We do not want to conquer the world. We do not want to impose our system on anybody else. We have fought three wars in the last 50 years. We haven't had an acre of territory out of it. We haven't gotten an economic concession. We have fought these wars - for what. Only so that others might have what we enjoy - independence, the right of people to be free, the right of the world to live at peace. This is what America wants, but this is

150

not what he wants. This is what our allies in the world want, but it is not what he wants.

Nixon went on to advocate for a strong military to keep the Soviet Union, and Krushchev at bay. Emphasizing that the U.S. had double the economic strength of the U.S.S.R. at the time, he quoted Khrushchev as saying, "'Mr. Nixon, we're going to catch you. We're behind now, and we know it, but,' he said, 'our system is better than yours. We're more determined than you are. You are simply living for the day when we are going to catch you, and we're going to catch you in seven years, and then we're going to pass you, and when we go by,' he says, 'we'll wave and say, Come along, follow us; do as we do or you will fall hopelessly behind.'"

Changing the subject, he added, "I suppose that coming to Fordham that I would be expected to talk about moral and spiritual strength, and now the gentlemen of the press and many of those who might tend to think that here's the political gimmick would say, 'Here it comes.'

"I know, too, that there is a tendency in this world in which we live to say, 'Look, we live in a tough world, in a hard world.'

"Khrushchev is tough. Mao Tse-tung is tough. What do they respect? Power only. Military power. Economic power. And, therefore, we've got to meet them militarily and economically, and if we do that, we will have it made."

"My friends, we've got to meet them militarily and economically, as I have indicated. We've got to have a firm diplomacy, as I have indicated. But that isn't enough. That isn't worthy of America. It isn't worthy of our ideas, because that's all they have, and to those that say moral and spiritual strength, the strength of our ideals don't count, let me say they again must read history because the tyrants, the militarists, and the materialists for centuries have underestimated the power of moral and spiritual strength and they have been brought down by it and they will be brought down again by it if we stand for it."

151

"And so, I say to all of the young people here, as you go out into the world, you will be lawyers and you will be doctors, and you will be teachers, and we want all of you to be successful, but remember: Strengthen America whenever you can by participation in the schools, in the churches, and in your own homes by reminding our people constantly of the mission - and we have it – and the destiny – and we have it – that America has in the world."

Speaking of the importance of foreign aid, he said, "We must make sure that a man like Khrushchev who has enslaved millions, a man like Khrushchev who has slaughtered thousands in the streets of Budapest, will not again be able to come to this country and point the finger to the United States and say, 'You are not practicing what you preach abroad.'

Let's do what we can, and you can help to do this as you go back to your communities, to right this situation."

Finally, Nixon concluded on a political note: "I can only say that we, those of us who might be selected to lead this country in the next four years, hope that we can be worthy of your trust and that we can hand America on to you not only strong militarily and economically, but, above all, strong in its heart, strong in its mind, strong in its soul, because this will be decisive. If you can keep America strong this way, we will win this struggle. We will win it not because of our military strength or our strength materially, but we will win it because we're on the right side, the side of freedom, the side of justice, the side of faith in God. These are the ideals that count and there are the things for which you and I must always live."

Nixon was concerned about the world at large, but there were perhaps greater concerns at home that would affect the university.

In the late 50's, the Bronx began its slide, largely attributed to Robert Moses, the great builder, who made the major blunder of splitting the Bronx in two with construction of the Cross Bronx

Expressway, believed to tear apart neighborhoods, causing thousands to flee. My own father, whose family home was just south of the new expressway on Nelson Avenue, was suddenly unable to walk north without crossing the huge divide created by the new roadway to the George Washington Bridge. His parents left in 1963, like so many other Italians and Jews who lived there, leading to the desolation that would last at least until the 1990's.

Photo: Fordham Law School

Father McGinley with Fordham Law Alumni Association Vice President, Thomas I. Sheridan (left), and Law Dean William Mulligan (right) in 1950.

As a result, the college at Rose Hill was in for a decade unlike any other in its history when the neighborhood, the once bucolic Manor Fordham, started to become a slum, to use a term common in the 50's and 60's.

Downtown was another story. Father McGinley signed the deed to buy the immense property at Lincoln Center on February 28, 1958 so Fordham could have a real Manhattan campus. The decaying building at 302 Broadway that Gannon had purchased was set for the wrecking ball, and the Law School and other graduate programs needed new space. Coincidentally, the Metropolitan Opera and the New York Philharmonic were also in need of new homes.

Moses and the city decided Lincoln Center, a depressed area of the city, would be the perfect home for a giant arts and educational complex. Father McGinley, whose father had been a friend to Moses, was at the right place at the right time.

As Father McGinley described it, one of his advisors, George Hammer suggested going to Moses. He said, "Go to see him and ask him if you can rent five floors in the Coliseum Building (the New York Coliseum [1956-2000], which was being built at the time). Tell him it's about the size you need and ask him if you could have the right to use the big Coliseum itself for major events of the university. Bob will turn that down. If he does agree to it, fine, but I don't think he will. I think what he will do is say 'why don't you let me bring you in on the Urban Development Program at 9th Avenue and 59th Street.'"

Sure enough, McGinley visited Moses in Babylon, Long Island and did exactly what was suggested. As predicted, Moses' response was, "No, you don't want that. It's not built for that purpose. It's built for offices. In schools everybody moves at the end of the class hour…Why don't you let me bring you in on the urban renewal project one block west of that?" Moses then asked, "Let's see. How much room would you need? Ten acres?"

McGinley said, "I almost fell off my chair. I was thinking about something about twice the size of the Vincent Building [302 Broadway]. When he mentioned acres, I couldn't believe it. I never heard anyone talk about New York City real estate in terms of acres."

Officially, the purchase of 320,230 square feet came as Fordham was made "collegiate sponsor" in the Lincoln Center Urban Renewal Project under Title 1 of the Housing Act of 1949. The acquisition cost the university $2,241,610. The federal government paid two-thirds the cost of the land and Fordham paid one third.

Fordham was at an advantage as the first sponsor to commit to participating in the project, which allowed the university to select its parcel. McGinley chose 60th to 62nd Streets from Columbus to Amsterdam Avenues, partly because the land was among the cheapest of the portions available. It was quite a deal and he was

154

even permitted to incorporate the name "Lincoln Center" into the official name of the new campus, which carried a certain cachet.

The city would condemn thousands of buildings considered sub-standard and unsanitary to commence building, leading to numerous delays. There were protests and a lawsuit filed by a group called "Protestants and Other Americans United for the Separation of Church and State." It claimed the city shouldn't be in business with a Catholic university.

After numerous court battles with a number of groups defending the thousands of tenants, homeowners and business owners who would be displaced by the condemnation, Robert Moses, who had many titles at the time, among them Chairman of the Committee on Slum Clearance, won. In 1959, McGinley announced his three-phase construction plan that would cost the university $25 million. Stage I was the Law School (completed in 1961). Stage two, scheduled for 1968, was a 14-story multi-purpose building and a three-story dramatic arts building. Stage three (1975) would be a high-rise building for future expansion and a communication arts building. As part of the project, the city was getting a new arts center and creating homes for the New York Philharmonic, the Metropolitan Opera and the New York City Ballet, among other entities.

Chapter X:
Vietnam and Campus Unrest

In May 1960, the Lincoln Center campus was dedicated with numerous national figures present. Cardinal Spellman, still Archbishop until his death in 1967, presided. He said, "This is the greatest thing that has happened to Fordham since my predecessor, Archbishop Hughes, built the university up at Rose Hill."

U.S. Supreme Court Justice Earl Warren gave the keynote address. Perhaps fearing negative press on account of the condemned property, Governor Nelson Rockefeller and Mayor Robert Wagner sent representatives. Robert Moses was there. He said, "We have had to fight for this campus as we have had to do battle for every good cause in this busy old city which resists change and has had more than its fair share of sensationalism, intolerance and bigotry. It is a great day for Fordham and for all of New York."

The Law School moved in as scheduled in 1961. Other academic programs previously at 302 Broadway relocated in 1969. More buildings were built over time.

Attorney General Robert F. Kennedy spoke at the dedication of the law school building on November 18, 1961. During his remarks, he said, "It is always an experience to come back to Fordham but it is particularly pleasant and non-partisan to appear following the Tuesday next after the first Monday in November [Election Day]. I am privileged to share with you such a special hour in Fordham's history. Also, I am honored to acquire, without travail, a full-fledged Fordham alumnus status. Perhaps the very first at Lincoln Square. We alumni must cooperate in the common cause. Moreover, I claim other ties to Fordham. Another Kennedy had his Cambridge credential legalized by Fordham. Many of my close associates at Justice are Fordham graduates and also, as Attorney General, I am privileged to be the largest single employer of Fordham law graduates in North America. This is due to a discriminating merit system, I assume. I must admit your Fordham lawyers always keep their eye on the ball. This is not easy, since the other eye is always on the next judicial vacancy. Quite a turnover."

Kennedy also said, "I am privileged to lie in the home once occupied by the late Robert H. Jackson, Justice of our Supreme Court. I am also honored to occupy the office he graced as Attorney General of the United States. He had every needed quality and attribute for these high offices and was besides a great advocate. It was always his strong conviction that the greatest attribute of a lawyer was courage. Today we can and need to subscribe to that belief. We can and need to believe that this edifice, conceived and brought to being by faith and courage, will instill in those who come to know it the courage to protect and defend what they stand for and represent.

"Courage will never be an elective in a course of studies here. Your own beloved Chief Justice [John T.] Loughran [Chief Judge of the New York Court of Appeals and a Fordham Law grad] was wont to say, 'The law is no place for the mealy mouth.' And beyond this hour and place and city I prayed that all of us will have that quality of mind which will enable us to meet danger and difficulties with faith and firmness. Let us, like the Lincoln honored here, have faith that right makes might, and in that faith, let us to the end, dare to do our duty, as we understand it." ("Right makes might" is a reversal of President Lincoln's famous phrase from his 1860 Cooper Union address on slavery.)

Simultaneous with the construction at Lincoln Center, Father McGinley built a new student center at Rose Hill at a cost of $4.1 million. It housed recreational facilities for students, including the Ramskellar, but there was no bowling alley as originally promised. (Years after it had been removed, the bowling alley in the basement of Queens Court was still missed by students who

157

knew it by reputation.) The building today, of course, is known as the McGinley Center.

The year 1962 was momentous in that Latin was removed as a requirement for those enrolled in Fordham College. It would go the way of the Ratio Studiorum, which was also a thing of the past. At first, students continued to take Latin as an elective, though they could now choose other foreign languages. Not surprisingly, the number of Latin students dwindled very steadily throughout the 60's, until it was no longer offered at all.

After a long run by Father McGinley, 1963 delivered a new president in Vincent T. O'Keefe, 43, who would preside for only two years, but who had been groomed to replace his predecessor. McGinley stepped down, still a young man at 57. O'Keefe didn't have much time to make changes, but he created a legacy nonetheless. He ended his years in office with a student body numbering 8,951, (1,836 of whom were in Fordham College) and he restored the football program.

O'Keefe has the distinction of bringing back a student run football team that operated independently of the university. Incredibly, the students were able to pull off a number of victories and actually earned the school some money thereafter.

Jim Lansing, who had been an All-American player for Fordham in the early 40's, was hired as coach. Lansing, a native of nearby Pelham and a graduate of its public high school, had been a star end in the aforementioned Cotton and Sugar Bowls for Fordham in the early 40's. Prior to the start of his senior season, he was called to the war and served in the Navy Air Corps as a fighter pilot. He returned to Fordham for the 1946 season, but injured his shoulder in the first game, ending his playing career. Lansing then served as an assistant coach from 1947 through 1954, when the university dropped football.

Several years after a six-year high school coaching stint in New Rochelle, Lansing returned to Fordham in 1964 as the new head coach. In eight seasons, he led the team to an overall record of

30–21–3. After ending his term as coach in 1971, he stayed at Fordham to serve as an assistant athletic director and the director of intramural athletics. He died in 2000 at the age of 81.

Father O'Keefe, the short-term caretaker, also oversaw the remodeling of Dealy Hall that delivered a huge, 60's-style computer to the university. He oversaw completion of Faculty Memorial Hall on Belmont Avenue, just outside the university gates. Originally a loft building, it was converted to offices and classrooms at a cost of $1.9 million. Plaques were placed in the lobby to commemorate illustrious professors. Father O'Keefe also built the parking lot on Southern Boulevard.

Harry Stanton, class of 1966, was managing editor of *The Ram* who went on to work at the *Associated Press* and later as an attorney, though he took a detour through the Marine Corps during the Vietnam War. He remembers the 1960's at Fordham as a time of immense change, ascribed partly to the Baby Boom, but also to Vietnam, the creation of Thomas More College and, surprisingly, the newly paved parking lot.

Stanton remembers arriving on campus in the fall of 1962 as the Beatles were recording their first song, "Love Me Do." Within only a few months, the idyllic era that song reflected gave way to various crises like the Cuban Missile Crisis, the beginning of U.S. involvement in Southeast Asia and the assassination of President Kennedy.

At Fordham in the early part of the decade, there was just a foreshadowing of what was to become much more heated by the end of the 60's, when the university truly became a center of political activism and countercultural activity, like Columbia and NYU.

First, on October 11, 1962, there was a visit from 34-year-old Madame Nhu (Trần Lệ Xuân), the titular First Lady of South Vietnam, who was the sister-in-law of the fallen South Vietnamese president, Ngo Dinh Diem. His overthrow was attributed to President Kennedy and the university's conservative faction, a large one, was supportive of Nhu causing a dispute on campus.

There were rumblings about traditional Catholic issues. Fordham was so conservative and dominated by the Jesuits, said Stanton, that a story in *The Ram* about the science behind the birth control pill caused the administration to confiscate every single copy of that issue delivered to campus, before any could be distributed to the student body.

One of the first real protests at Fordham happened when the Southern Boulevard parking lot was paved. The university was promoting the idea of commuting by car, partly because the neighborhood was changing and it was getting increasingly dangerous to take the subway. But, it imposed a fee to park, hence the protests and a short-lived boycott.

The leadership at Fordham, but not necessarily the Jesuits, realized they had to make certain adjustments to a school that until this time had been a pseudo-seminary. It was realized that the university needed to become something more akin to the bigger colleges and universities throughout the U.S. Enrollment at this time was on the rise because the first Baby Boomers born in 1946 were turning 18, but Fordham was also competing for students with the newly introduced New York State university system (SUNY) and expansion at schools like Iona College and St. John's University.

First, there were small changes like a "three-three" program, so Fordham Prep students could complete high school and college in six years. The Lincoln Center College of Liberal Arts was established. It would require that every student have a social action project involving the poor. The world-known cultural anthropologist Margaret Mead was hired to teach. Sociologist Fr. Andrew Greeley, later a best-selling fiction author, was also brought on.

Rock 'n' Roll came to Fordham with performances in the gym by Peter, Paul and Mary, the Kingston Trio and the Beach Boys. The first reports of drug use on campus also came at this time.

But life at Rose Hill was disrupted forever with the inception of Thomas More College for women. It opened in 1964 with 213 freshmen; many claimed it was a response to the need to compete and to fill classrooms.

There was actually speculation that women were admitted to avoid what happened when World Wars I and II broke out and so many men left college to enlist. With Vietnam on the horizon, Harry Stanton said, "They [the administration] were hedging their bets because the draft could devastate them. Women were an insurance policy."

Father John Donohue, Fordham class of 1939, the first dean of Thomas More, disputed that charge in the university's Sesquicentennial Oral History Project. "When it looked like there would be a new college admitting both men and women and that the first class would have 1,000 members, some cynics said what they were planning was a college for dollars, dolls and dokes," said Donohue. He claimed that was not the case. There would be a separate college and the academic requirements would be as stringent, or more so, than those for Fordham College. Unlike other women's colleges, like Barnard, where the women's and men's divisions held separate classes, Fordham's coeds attended class with their male counterparts, which is likely why Thomas More was absorbed so quickly into Fordham College in 1974.

"This college was going to enroll…gifted, highly qualified young women, but young women from middle-class families of German-American, Irish-American, Italian-American, and Polish-American backgrounds who would be the first of their families to go to college," said Father Donohue. "In order to reassure their parents that this was a safe and trustworthy environment, they chose as the first dean, somebody who looked like Cardinal

161

Spellman, and thereby could reassure the parents and project a kind of sound image," he said of himself.

Father O'Keefe said, "Fordham College was a male precinct, as it were, and there was no idea of introducing young ladies there. In the eyes of many people, especially the Jesuits, Fordham University really was Fordham College. We said, let's try it this way...the first two years we really had a mix of extraordinary students who proved every bit as intelligent and productive as the young men, and I think they had a good influence on the men. It wasn't like soothing the savage beast or anything like that, but it was a good influence. The students were excellent so that after a time the fears about Fordham College were allayed and eventually the two schools merged into the coeducational Fordham College."

The first women were actually more advanced scholastically than their male counterparts in Fordham College; they had a median SAT score 36 points higher than that of the men.

The name Thomas More (not a Jesuit) was chosen because of the great Brit's dedication to the synthesis of faith and science. And, according to Father Donohue, Thomas More had gone to great troubles to educate his daughters. He emphasized the liberal arts as a great model for the Christian gentleman.

In the tradition of Archbishop Hughes who had hired his brother-in-law to design Fordham's first buildings, the director of admissions for Thomas More turned out to be the niece of Father O'Keefe. A redheaded woman, she bore a striking resemblance to her uncle, the president (who also had red hair), though no complaints were aired. Anne O'Keefe determined that the first women at Thomas More would have a certain character. According to Father Schroth, she declared that there would be no nuns, as she would not have the place resemble a convent. Married women would be accepted, and female students could get married. Working mothers, however, need not apply. And, though looks would not be a factor in admission, neatness, poise and personality definitely counted.

By 1966, Father Donohue had been replaced as dean of Thomas More by Dr. Patricia Plante, 33. Plante was the first woman to have been appointed as an undergraduate dean in the history of the university. She served until 1968 and was eventually married to a former Fordham Jesuit.

According to Stanton, there was no overt prejudice against the "coeds" from neither the students nor the Jesuit faculty, but there were rumblings. Editorials in *The Ram* alluded to good grades for females who had nice legs. At first, women weren't allowed to work at *The Ram*, purportedly because the paper was an instrument of Fordham College, not Thomas More. In the end, Stanton said, the men at Fordham were probably more gaga over football than they were over the coeds sitting next to them in class, and business as usual prevailed.

Stanton's feelings about minimal bias against women were confirmed by several Thomas More graduates interviewed.

Gerri Cunningham Paré, a retired journalist, was a member of the first class that entered in 1964 and a first to enter the communication department's newly established film program. Her memories are almost universally positive.

Paré said the ratio of men to women was about 50 to one, but the women were treated well by the Jesuits, the lay teachers and even their classmates. "The Jesuits demanded the best from you, but the vast majority were intellectually stimulating and they made you think," she said.

She remembered a warm welcome during the first few days, but noted that sometimes the Jesuits and other instructors forgot or ignored the fact that there were women in class.

"One Jesuit," she recalled, "told us, 'If you are majoring in the sciences, I want you to get involved in the humanities and vice versa, because I want you to be Renaissance men.'" Even though she would never be such a man, Gerri took that to heart by getting a job at the Bronx Zoo during one summer to counterbalance her communications studies.

"It really was quite nice. I felt the fellows were very receptive. We were assigned 'older brothers' from the junior class and they were supposed to look out for us," said Paré. She added that she felt she received a fine and well-rounded education and made lasting friendships that have been consistent in her life. "The campus was very welcoming, even loving," said Paré. "I have friends I made there to this day." Since graduation, like so many other Fordham students, classmates helped her find more than one of the jobs she held during her career.

There were minor issues, however. At first, there was an absence of athletic teams for women. Women's basketball was added fairly quickly, but the next sport, women's tennis, didn't arrive until 1973.

The male cheerleaders at Fordham did not easily welcome females to the squad. At first they insisted on a group called the "Fordham Precision Dancers" that would supplement the cheerleaders during basketball and football games.

According to George Seuffert who conducted the Fordham University Band from 1951 through the 80's, Father Harold Mulqueen, then the band moderator, was not too enthused about signing up women. Seuffert said when the inevitable happened and "young ladies" applied for membership, "I'll never forget Father's reaction! There's still a picture in the Band Room of the boys standing around the table, grinning from ear to ear, and Father signing up this young lady for the band and Father's expression was, 'I guess I have to do it, but I don't have to like it.'"

Paré, through a comical incident, was instrumental in getting women admitted to the swimming pool in the basement of the gym. "In freshman year," she said, "we weren't allowed to use the pool. Guys used the pool and didn't wear swimsuits. I got that rule changed. One terribly rainy day, a friend and I were trying to get to the gym to buy tickets to a Beach Boys concert."

Instead of heading outside from the McGinley Center, they walked into the glass corridor that connected the two buildings.

"As we entered the gym building, we saw a naked man with a towel around his neck. He screamed louder than we did," said Paré.

"Someone relayed the incident to *The Ram*, which reported the story. In no time, there was a policy that all swimmers had to wear swimsuits and, soon after, women were allowed to use the pool. I certainly didn't set out to be an instrument of change, but I was." (The Lombardi Center had not yet been built at this time; the only pool was the one in the gym.)

It was during that first year of Thomas More that Father O'Keefe also made a huge decision to abandon the idea of having Alabama Governor George Wallace speak at Fordham. Wallace was, of course, an incendiary figure who had famously attempted in 1963 to stop four black students from enrolling in four separate elementary schools in Huntsville in his state.

"What had developed in the meantime (from the time Wallace was booked until the time the speech was called off)," said Father O'Keefe, "was that terrible bombing and fire in the church in Birmingham, Alabama, in which several people were killed. Wallace would have appeared at Fordham in the 'American Age' series not even a week after that terrible tragedy. The local police called and said if he comes to campus we'll need every policeman in New York City. I thought since this would have represented a great risk to the whole community, I called it off, for which we were sacked in the press. If I had to do it again, today, I would do the same thing."

Not long after came the start of the formal U.S. involvement in Vietnam. Many members of the class of 1965 enlisted or were drafted into the armed services. They had not yet realized the risks involved in Vietnam and were not part of the next wave

165

who started seeking deferments. Stanton reported hearing immediately about friends who had died, including track star Frank Tomeo (class of 1963) who went into the Marines, was serving in a helicopter unit and wrote a letter to his fellow alumni expressing that he couldn't wait to land "in country." He believed, as many others did, that the Americans would straighten Vietnam out in short order and return very quickly.

Frank Casey, an editor of *The Ram*, was killed on his 30th day of service in Vietnam. Ronald Golebiewski, the paper's sports editor, was also killed very soon after arriving.

The Vietnam Veterans Memorial Plaque that hangs in the Rose Hill Gym displays the names and bronzed photographs of 20 of the 23

Photo: Fordham University

Father McShane dedicated the Vietnam Veterans Memorial Plaque in the University Church in 2013.

Fordham men (three more were identified after the memorial was erected) who died in that conflict, though not all died in Vietnam. Lt. Col. Bruce A. Laue of the New York Army National Guard wrote in *Fordham Magazine* that Walter Francis Burke (class of 1962) was shot down over Laos. Edward Stephen Krukowski (class of 1960) was killed in Cambodia. Robert Charles Murray (class of 1968) died in 1970 near the village of Hiep Duc by throwing himself onto an explosive device in order to save his comrades. It was an act "above and beyond the call of duty," which led to his Medal of Honor.

"It tells the story of the war," said an emotional Lt. Col. Frank Licameli (class of 1978) of the memorial at its 2004 dedication.

William J. Burke Sr. (class of 1968), who, with several classmates was the driving force behind the memorial, said, "It took time [for us to honor our fellow alumni], but we did it."

More recently, another memorial was dedicated in the University Church.

"None of our 23 classmates wanted to die, but they were willing to and that's what makes them special," said retired U.S. Army Gen. John M. (Jack) Keane, class of 1966. "They were willing to put at risk everything they cared about—and for what? A simple yet profound sense of duty. This is true honor and we can never, ever take that kind of devotion for granted."

For Keane, a retired four-star general and a former vice chief of staff of the Army, the 23 men were soldiers of extraordinary valor. Among them were two Medal of Honor recipients, Father Vincent R. Capodanno (class of 1952), and the noted Robert Murray. They included winners of a Distinguished Service Cross, an Air Force Cross, two Silver Stars, and two Bronze Stars. They died between 1964 and 1973; all but one served as an officer.

The Vietnam memorial resides in the narthex of the University Church, close to the 230 names of Fordham alumni who died in World War II.

By late 1965, when Father O'Keefe was called to Rome to serve as a secretary to the Jesuit Superior General, Father Leo McLaughlin was chosen as president of Fordham. He had been chairman of the communication arts department, dean of Fordham College and had studied at Georgetown and the University of Paris. When he was installed on April 5, 1966, he promised a "revolution" at Fordham at a time when the university was turning 125 years old.

Frank Corbin, whose long connection to Fordham as an alumnus and part-time faculty member gave him an historical perspective, believed Father Leo Plowden McLaughlin was a major source of change in the 1960's. With colleagues Father George J. McMahon (dean of Fordham College from 1962 to

167

1974), Father Donohue, who headed Thomas More College and others, he led the university through a time of somber and sobering difficulty and evolution.

Father McLaughlin was already a legend at Fordham by the time he ascended to the presidency. Students loved him because he spent time with them and listened. He was forward thinking, a media man in the tradition of Father Gannon, without the extreme conservative opinions. His secretary, Stella Moundas, had worked for him from his days as dean through his presidency. She said, "He was a very dynamic dean who was extremely popular with the students. In addition to his responsibilities as dean, he taught English and oversaw senior retreats. He was clearly gifted as an instructor. He felt it essential that a teacher be loved by his students."

McLaughlin oversaw a lifting of the dress code. Men were no longer expected to wear jackets and ties. The Ramskeller started to sell beer, since the drinking age at that time was 18. Liquor was even allowed in the dorms, though men and women could not stay overnight in the same room.

In response to internal demands for a more "liberalized" curriculum, the university created Bensalem College in 1967. An experimental college with no set requirements and no grades, it was studied by a wide array of educators and reported on by such large-circulation publications of the day as *Look, Esquire*, and the *Saturday Review*. Faculty and students lived together in an old building on 191st Street in the Bronx. It was a short-lived experiment. The school closed in 1974.

During McLaughlin's years, the communication arts department morphed into the communications department and one of the boldest, most introspective media thinkers of the decade became a short-term professor, the great Marshall McLuhan.

Dr. Philip Freund was another well-remembered professor of communications who stayed from 1959 to 1979 and knew the

168

McLuhan story from the beginning. A World War II veteran who had been assigned to the Training Film Branch (perhaps with Ronald Reagan), he became a scriptwriter for NBC at $35 per script. He convinced Fordham to hire him to teach writing, but only radio at first. "I told Father St. George (then department head) 'There's really no point in teaching radio writing; it's a dying field. Why don't we teach television?' He said, 'We've no equipment.' I told him, 'I can teach the subject without it; all I need is a blackboard.'"

Dr. Freund said the communications department was looked down upon as not truly academic. "All this changed very suddenly when New York State set up funding for distinguished visiting professorships, including the Albert Schweitzer Chair in Humanities, which was granted to Fordham, but soon rescinded because of the separation of church and state. Fordham, nevertheless continued with the idea, using its own money, and a newly arrived Jesuit in the department, Father John Culkin, had the idea of granting this professorship for one year to Marshall McLuhan.

McLuhan was author of the wildly popular *Understanding Media: The Extension of Man*, which became a cult classic. A Canadian who had spent most of his career in Canada, McLuhan all of a sudden became a popular American talk show guest, popping up regularly on *The Tonight Show* with Johnny Carson, the *David Susskind Show* and others. His famous quote, "The Medium is the Message," was discussed in countless venues.

In 1967, McLuhan, then 55, arrived at Fordham. His family was set up in a house in Bronxville and he was paid $100,000. He taught two courses, a seminar for 15 seniors and a huge class for more than 100 held in Keating Hall's first floor lecture hall.

John Phelan, Ph.D., a 1954 Fordham grad who was a professor and became longtime chairman of the communications department, remembered the large lecture as a cross between a comedy show and the Charlie Rose program on PBS. Guests were brought in to speak. There was lively, interesting discussion that sometimes turned chaotic. "It would go from one extreme to the other, from bad to great," said Phelan.

Some of the chaos, unfortunately, could later be explained by the fact that McLuhan was diagnosed with a brain tumor, which cut his time at Fordham short. McLuhan had an operation and eventually recovered, but he had missed a good part of the year. He did make a mark on Fordham and its students. There had also been a great deal of publicity during his short tenure.

The McLuhan episode was one of many high points for the communications department in those days, which Dr. Freund credited with turning the department around. All of a sudden, it became very popular and later became the biggest department for undergraduates. One teacher, considered legendary and beloved by many students, was Ed Walsh who was the Patterson Professor of Journalism from the 50's until the mid-70's.

Norma Vavolizza, class of 1969, who has had a distinguished career in communications, remembered Walsh as a mentor, advocate and friend.

"After graduation he did two unforgettable things. He recommended me for a job that advanced me into a Fordham network that has paid many dividends over the years—not just in terms of my career, but also in valued and now life-long friendships. Secondly, while he was ill and in fact dying, he managed to write a letter of recommendation to George Washington University's School of Public & International Affairs where I had applied for a graduate degree. He wouldn't let a student down, not ever. Whenever I am on campus and have the time, I stop by Robert's Hall to spend a moment before the commemorative stone that sits outside that old, dusty basement office of his, once hopelessly overtaken by books, newspapers, stacks of paper and ash trays. The conversations we had there amidst the haze of cigarette smoke helped launch my career and eternal love for the purpose and role of journalism."

170

Vavolizza spoke very highly of another professor, Louis A. Boccardi, who became managing editor of the *Associated Press*. In the 60's, he taught undergraduate journalism at Fordham. "Once we learned the basic principles of good reporting, Lou had us call into the *AP* once a week and take an assignment off the daybook [a calendar of events for coverage] along with his real-life reporters. Copy had to be postmarked that day (yes, snail mail!). In the spring of 1968, I was assigned to cover Mayor John Lindsay at City Hall, and a fluff piece – a group of Rockettes taking judo lessons at the Latin Quarter. But there were two other assignments I'll never forget. One was a press conference in New York given by Dr. Martin Luther King, weeks before his assassination in Memphis. Shortly after that assignment, I was sent to cover a press conference given by Robert Kennedy who was in the middle of a contentious campaign for the presidency. Weeks after, RFK, too, lost his life. He would have been the commencement speaker that June on Rose Hill for the class of 1968."

The Kennedy speech was an ill-fated, yet highly anticipated event. The date would have been June 8, 1968. Kennedy was killed by Sirhan Sirhan at the Ambassador Hotel in Los Angeles on the evening of June 5th; he died the next day. Father McLaughlin was heard to reveal later that the last phone call Bobby Kennedy made in his life was to him, to assure the university president that despite his primary wins that night, virtually assuring him the Democratic presidential nomination, he would be at Fordham that Saturday for his speech.

Gerri Paré, Thomas More class of 1968, remembered what was supposed to be the celebratory day of her graduation and the days before, which would normally have been full of hope, pride and joy. Paré said RFK held a special place in her heart because three years earlier Kennedy's office in the Justice Department had intervened to save the salaries of a few Thomas More students, including hers, when a major publisher refused to pay the students after they were hired for the summer to sell a set of encyclopedias published by the entity. Paré said:

"My family was assembled, ready to head to Fordham from our home near the Bronx neighborhood of Parkchester, but I resisted. Grief stricken by the events of the last few days, such a celebration seemed out of place; our keynote speaker had just been murdered. But, I was the first in my generation to earn a college degree. I realized I couldn't indulge my emotions and deprive everyone in my family of such a moment.

"Three mornings earlier I had awakened with delight at the prospect of that night's senior prom. On special days, Mom would come in to wake me with a giddy 'Wake up it's your birthday!' or 'Happy Easter,!' so I expected her to be smiling, set to tell me the big day had arrived. Instead, she was somber. She said, 'They shot him; they shot Bobby Kennedy!' No, it couldn't be happening again, I thought, remembering too well the days we learned President Kennedy and Martin Luther King, Jr. had been killed.

"Though swept off my feet by my hunky date, Ken, the evening at the Waldorf Astoria (complete with music, dancing and long-stemmed roses), turned sour when he took me home. Back at my doorstep, Ken, a fourth-year Cornell medical student, offered what he was hearing, that Bobby Kennedy's condition was 'extremely grave.' There was virtually no chance of survival. That very hour, Senator Kennedy died.

"I can't say my prom had been ruined, but death was in the air and we all felt such a loss. Graduation parties and Saturday's ceremony held no appeal."

In place of a celebratory graduation, Fordham held a somber distribution of diplomas immediately followed by a funeral High Mass for RFK. "It seemed appropriate to be in a sea of black gowns and mortarboards," said Paré. "1968 was such a tumultuous year, with student revolts, Martin Luther King's assassination, riots in the streets, protests against the Vietnam War and now this latest atrocity."

"As we were departing the campus, we learned Kennedy's body had begun to wend its way slowly by train from New York to Washington, D.C. for his burial at Arlington National Cemetery, near his brother the president. Throngs of people lined the tracks all along the route.

"My B.A. degree in one hand, a huge bouquet of multicolored daisies from my parents in the other, I accepted congratulations from friends and family. But the rest of the day is a blank. Did we go out to eat or to a family party? I don't recall. All I remember is the melancholy déjà vu when we all settled in front of the TV watching the live coverage from Washington, just as we had one long weekend five years earlier."

A year later on June 7, 1969, RFK's younger brother, Senator Ted Kennedy (D-Mass) was there on Edwards Parade to give the address that eluded his brother. With little small talk, he got right to the heart of the day's number one issues, the military industrial complex, cost overruns and misspending at the Pentagon, Vietnam and the toll all of that was taking here at home – riots, poverty and all around neglect. Decades later, his words sound like they came from a conservative.

"Today we are paying the price of inattention to domestic needs. The price is high. It is paid in riots, crime, welfare payments, poor housing, pollution and the growing divisions of our people," said Kennedy. "Unless we adjust our policies, our cities will continue to suffer – not because of a nuclear attack, but because of poison in the air, or warfare in the streets.

"Faced with these enormous problems, does it make more sense to spend more on bombs alone in Vietnam than we spend on primary and secondary education? To spend nearly as much on cost overruns on a single new type of airplane – C5A –as the entire nation spends on its police? To spend some $15 million on an air defense network – the SAGE system – which never worked properly and is now being abandoned? To be asked to spend three-quarters of a billion dollars for 'rent' for our bases in Spain, when if we are protecting Spain, it should be paying us?

"But we cannot do so if we overkill on one, and underfund on the other. We cannot maintain a budget for defense that satisfies each service, each contractor, each Congressman. The American people will not continue to pay this price - and I do not believe they should.

"As our nation is threatened from without – so it is threatened from within. As we face uncertainty in the world, we face it equally at home.

"How are we to balance these needs? Who will make the case for the total well-being of America, if not the representatives of new Americans? In the current debate, I believe the burden of proof is on those who seek to justify spending two-thirds of all controllable tax dollars on defense from enemies abroad. We know our country is troubled. We know part of the problem is that our domestic programs are starved for funds. Yet when we ask for justifications for defense programs, we get slogans, not logic; we get scare not reason.

"In particular, we should realize now, when we have a rough parity of nuclear arms with the Soviets, we have the best possible opportunity to negotiate an agreement on strategic arms limitations. We were ready to begin last year, but we felt it more important to show our deep distaste for the Soviet invasion of Czechoslovakia. There is much we do not know about Soviet intentions, and more we do not understand. We must proceed with caution. But I believe we would enhance our chances for security – not endanger them – if, this summer, we suspend deployment of our anti-ballistic missile system and delay flight tests of our multiple warheads for a fixed time while we try again to begin arms control talks with the Russians.

"If we let this moment pass, our adversaries may decide to take a giant step in the arms race themselves. The case for restraint on our part would be gravely weakened. But if we seize the moment, we may find that they, as we are ready to steer away from an ever escalating arms race."

Senator Kennedy's Fordham address came just 31 days before the infamous incident at Chappaquiddick.

President Nixon was also going to speak at Rose Hill in 1969, but a student protest and sit-in on the route Nixon's car would have taken through the campus forced the White House to cancel the speech.

Protests and unrest continued.

The Ad Hoc Committee of Fordham University Students Against the War recruited more than 100 students to join a Vietnam War rally in Central Park in April 1967.

The following November, Students for a Democratic Society (SDS) threatened to block air force personnel from recruiting on campus.

The university's executive vice president at this time was Father Timothy Healy who went on to fame as president of Georgetown University and as head of the New York Public Library. He, alongside Father McLaughlin, weathered the storm of controversy during these years. Healy made his name at Fordham, first as head of WFUV and later as a vice president. He was instrumental in keeping what shred of peace existed. His departure in 1969 was a blow.

Just before the 1968 Christmas break, there were protests virtually every day as students sat-in at Lincoln Center, the McGinley Center or the Administration Building. One day, during a hunger strike, there was violence over the university's effort to deny financial aid to students who participated in disturbances on campus.

Still another protest occurred over demands to admit more Black and Puerto Rican students. Dean of Student Affairs Martin J. Meade, who was 37, was barricaded in his office during a meeting with students and later had a heart attack, which some ascribed to the incident.

On December 4, 1968, nearly a dozen African-American student demonstrators barricaded Meade in his office by propping a desk up against his door. Compared to similar campus demonstrations happening around the country, the demonstration was "quick and orderly," wrote *The New York Times*, noting that "one solidly built Negro youth . . . stood before the inside door" demanding that demonstrators use ashtrays and not put cigarette ashes on the floor.

That "solidly built youth," Quinton Wilkes, Ph.D., GSAS '69, recalled that the demonstration also received coverage in *Time* magazine and in *The Ram*. Although dubbed a "militant action," Wilkes said that two of the student leaders had actually made an appointment to speak with Meade, who had always said he was never held against his will. (Dr. Wilkes, who later taught at Fordham, was the first black male student to earn a doctorate in psychology at the university.)

The group demanded that Meade sign a document urging the university not to cut off federal aid to black students who protest peacefully. Other demands emerged in the days that followed, including the implementation of an African- American studies curriculum. One year later, the Institute for African American Studies was launched; it later became the Department of African and African American Studies.

"Marty Meade was very instrumental in developing the institute, and I think that says a lot about his character," said Wilkes.

The unrest didn't stop there. At one point, a fake bomb was planted in a desk in the Administration Building. Dr. Andrew B. Myers, an alumnus and professor, said, "I was president of the Faculty Senate at the time, and my office was in that building. My secretary was a grand older lady, a feisty gal, Mrs. Rose

Pierce, who came from the Italian-American colony across Fordham Road. She took no nonsense from anybody, including whoever happened to be signing the letters she typed.

"I was in class one morning, early, when I heard a kind of uproar outside. I continued teaching until the end of the hour, at which point I discovered that when Rose got in that morning, she opened her desk drawer and found what looked exactly like a bomb. A cruel trick, unworthy of Fordham. You might have expected her to faint or run to the far end of the building and get out screaming. Not Rose. She resolutely picked up the bomb – the police later determined that it was a fake – and stomped out of the building with people dodging her in all directions, she muttering words no one knew the lady knew beforehand, and flung the contraption on the lawn to blow up if it chose."

In March of 1968 there was a rally in front of the gym led by Fr. Philip Hurley, moderator of the LaFarge Society dedicated to studying injustice toward African Americans protesting the exclusion of blacks from some groups marching in the St. Patrick's Day Parade. Some students even joined Martin Luther King's march in Selma, Alabama.

(The irony that a number of members of the Nixon administration were Fordham alumni was noted by many. Among them were: John Mitchell, the president's notorious Attorney General (Fordham Law), William Casey, chairman of the Securities and Exchange Commission and later President Reagan's CIA director, and the aforementioned G. Gordon Liddy.)

Father McLaughlin had a lot to contend with during those very turbulent years. Though he was able to advance the university in many ways by making it more liberal, to keep pace with the times, he also introduced traditions like the awards presentation for graduating seniors called Encaenia and the Fordham Club, a specially chosen group of 20 to 30 outstanding seniors.

In the end, however, financial problems and the resistance to change by the elders caught up with him. Fordham was in serious debt. In September of 1967, McLaughlin announced that there was a deficit of $1 million. Construction at Lincoln Center and some on Rose Hill (a new chemistry building, named John Mulcahy Hall for the donor, renovations to Collins, Duane Library and Larkin Hall) was costing $62 million. The projected cost of $25 million at Lincoln Center had also been greatly underestimated. By 1968, the deficit would rise to more than $3.7 million. Fiscal troubles and decreased enrollment, coupled with the fact that the old guard of Jesuits saw McLaughlin as the agent for their loss of control of the university, meant the president would be gone by December 1968.

Dejected, McLaughlin left the Jesuits and married a family friend. He took a teaching job at Ramapo College of New Jersey. Though his wife was younger, he outlived her and eventually returned to Fordham to spend the final years of his life among his Jesuit brothers. When he died in 1996, *The New York Times* wrote the following:

"Dr. McLaughlin was the Jesuit answer to the 1960's. As a transforming president of Fordham from 1965 to 1969, he opened up the curriculum beyond traditional theological courses, encouraged academic experimentation, fought for higher faculty salaries even as he was turning the established Jesuit faculty inside out, brought Marshall McLuhan to Fordham as a professor and even wrested the university from Jesuit control. If he shocked some Jesuit sensibilities, Dr. McLaughlin had given fair warning. As a pupil at the Jesuit-run Loyola prep school in Manhattan, for example, he was so highly visible, a classmate once recalled, that just about any time a student looked up from his books he would see Leo McLaughlin being ordered out 'for doing or saying something dangerous.'"

By this time, as *The Times* mentioned, the Fordham Board of Trustees had a majority of lay people for the first time in its history, the result of a reorganization foretelling even more change for the future of the university.

Chapter XI:
Lean Years in the 70's and 80's

The new decade would start with a completely different culture and a new president, Fr. Michael P. Walsh, S.J., who had been president of the Board of Trustees, who once implied that he took a bullet for the university by agreeing to take the job.

The reorganized board with a majority of non-clerical members officially made the university an independent institution. A report was commissioned by the trustees to recommend what a church-related university had to do to become a "completely independent institution of higher learning." The 212-page document was issued in 1970 under the name, "The Sectarian College and the Public Purse." Fordham could no longer be called a Catholic college, officially at least, as was the national trend among other Catholic colleges and universities. In order to preserve aid from New York State, as dictated by the state's Blaine amendment forbidding direct government aid to educational institutions with any religious affiliation, Fordham was now officially non-sectarian.

The Jesuit community was incorporated separately from the university, as was Fordham Prep. The crucifixes that long hung in each of the school's hundreds of classrooms were eventually removed. If ever there was a moment for Archbishop Hughes to have rolled over in his grave, this was it. The University Church was allowed to remain because it was essentially a chapel.

Father Walsh was taking the first steps toward restoring the university's solvency. He hired an economist as executive vice president, worked with the faculty budget committee to cut the budget and accepted the counsel of the chairman of W.R. Grace and Company, Felix E. Larkin. Larkin, also chairman of the university's Board of Trustees, would spend his weekends at

Rose Hill helping with the books. By 1970, there was a budget surplus of $2 million.

Fiscal stability didn't stop the unrest on campus.

In October 1969, there had been a peaceful anti-Vietnam rally on Edwards Parade, featuring U.S. Senators Charles Goodel and Jacob Javits, Mayor John Lindsay, Congressman Allard Lowenstein and author, David Halberstam. Even Father Walsh participated, saying, "Our military engagement now stands as a denial of so much that is best in our society."

Just weeks later, things started to get heated. Students who were blocked from taking over the ROTC offices in Faculty Memorial Hall marched across campus and stormed the Administration Building.

"The New York Police were about in plain clothes and more police were available on buses just off campus," said then Academic Vice President Paul Reiss. "We felt that in addition to talking with the students that we must, in fact, get them out one way or another, hopefully in a peaceful manner. We tried to do that by utilizing Fordham's own security people.

"In hindsight, that was probably a mistake. The sight of a security officer wedging a bar between the door and frame between the hallway and the president's office while students were pushing up against the other side and throwing water at the security people was a terrible kind of sight. One wondered what one was getting to in the whole nature of higher education."

That demonstration was broken up when the NYPD arrested six students, charging them with trespassing.

In November, there was more of a flare-up when the arrested students, known as the Fordham Five (the charges were dropped against one) went to trial. The prosecutor was none other than Burton Roberts, who later became a famous judge and model for the character of Judge Myron Kovitsky in Tom Wolfe's "The Bonfire of the Vanities." The five were convicted and received suspended sentences.

181

The next April, the denial of tenure to a favored professor, Ronald Friedland of the English department, prompted violence when students again took over the Administration Building, this time occupying it for two days. A compromise between the students and Father Walsh was worked out, resulting in establishment of the Rose Hill Campus Council, which was to foster communication and understanding among the administration, faculty and students.

Less than a month later, peace on campus was interrupted yet again when President Nixon invaded Cambodia. That's when Kent State erupted with the killing of four students by the National Guard. At Fordham, there were no injuries, but students set a fire in the Campus Center that burned for four or more hours. The administration had to decide whether or not to hold final exams or to send all the students home. They resolved to let individual teachers decide how to end their classes.

According to Dr. Freund of the communications department, "the emotional impact of that was very strong, and at Fordham, the administration beat a steady retreat. Up to that point there had been a dress code and many rules of conduct, which now were abandoned. Students were given much more input; they demanded a say about the syllabus and, in our department, they even asked for a voice in the hiring of teachers. John Phelan, the chairman, met this skillfully by calling a meeting and explaining that the department was about to take in new professors, but if the candidates had to undergo an interrogation or catechism by the students, top-rate people would not apply. The students, convinced that he had a point, quickly gave way."

During this period of activism the university's African and African American Studies Department, one of the first black studies departments in the nation, was founded. It also saw the birth of *The Paper*, the alternative student newspaper that had a more leftist stance than *The Ram*. A faculty senate was also begun.

Father Walsh led Fordham through a turbulent time that was cut short in 1972. Walsh desperately wanted to return to Boston where he had been president of Boston College for 10 years. He was also said to have developed a heart condition, possibly due to the mounting stress of the job.

Felix Larkin, the board chairman, headed the search committee for a new president. Larkin had been general counsel to the U.S. Department of Defense under President Truman and was at this time still heading W.R. Grace. A Fordham grad from the early part of the century, he would not bow to the pressure to install a non-Jesuit university president and put out feelers for candidates at all 28 Jesuit colleges and universities in the U.S. It was a tough process. Out of 60 candidates, a number said no. Finally, those interested were narrowed down to Father Don Monan, professor of philosophy at Le Moyne College (later president of Boston College), and Father James Finlay, dean of the Fordham Graduate School of Arts and Sciences, and a former political science professor. Finlay didn't want the job either, but nevertheless made an impressive presentation to the board.

"They couldn't pick between them," said Larkin of his fellow board members. "We had a vote all day. We had six votes. It was like electing the Pope. We couldn't get a two-thirds majority for either one of them." When they finally decided on Finlay, they couldn't find him; he was not waiting by the phone, but had gone to visit his secretary in the hospital.

Finlay took on a big job and did it admirably, if not enthusiastically. The sad fact was that New York City was going bankrupt. The once glittering metropolis was now characterized by strikes, crumbling roadways, subway cars blanketed with graffiti (and lots more) and a high crime rate under the failed mayoralties of John Lindsay and Abe Beame. The Bronx was not a place parents wanted to send their children. They certainly didn't want their children traveling through the worst parts of the borough to get to Fordham, still an oasis amid the chaos.

183

Those who did come to Fordham did so because it was convenient and affordable, but nevertheless a step up from the city, state and other local Catholic schools. Fordham's reputation from the past carried it through this period. The student body, still mostly commuters, came almost exclusively from the five boroughs and counties to the north, east and west. Even those in the dorms were local kids, many from Brooklyn and Staten Island. Few had grown up farther away than Massachusetts or New Jersey.

Like thousands before and after him, Paul Phelan, class of 1982, now director of contracts for the New York City Human Resources Administration, put it this way: "As an Irish Catholic and product of Bronx Catholic schools - St. Brendan's Elementary, Mount Saint Michael Academy High School - my enrollment at Fordham was almost a foregone conclusion," though he did consider other colleges.

Also echoing so many interviewed for this book, Phelan spoke lovingly of his four years. "Fordham had it all and I didn't know I was missing anything. The mix of students worked. The differences melted into deeper understandings and acceptances. Fordham provided education, not just academic, but life education too. There were more than just Irish/Italians Catholics in the Bronx! My years at Fordham prepared me to go out into the world."

The 30th president, Finlay (1972-83), 49, was a low key Jesuit whose personality was a huge departure from the robust public personalities of his predecessors - and his two successors to date, though many spoke of him as a wonderfully warm individual, which didn't necessarily come through in public. Born in Ireland, he was raised in New York and attended Fordham for two years before getting his undergraduate degree from Loyola Chicago and a doctorate from Duke. Stella Moundas, who had been secretary to Fathers McLaughlin, Walsh, Finlay and, later, O'Hare, said Finlay was "the most enjoyable because he had such an even disposition. I found him warm and friendly. For example, he just loved Christmas. Every Christmas there was a wonderful party for the staff, alive with holiday spirit."

An unassuming former professor, Finlay described his own installation as low-key. "With Fordham still wrestling its way through a difficult financial period in the early 70's, the absence of pomp and ceremony seemed just right to me. I remember driving out to the airport with my distinguished and greatly liked predecessor, Michael Walsh, S.J., who was headed for Boston and his new duties there. Just before boarding his plane, Mike handed me the keys to his car, and that was that. Except for a brief introduction of me during commencement as the next Fordham president, the transfer of an ignition key marked my official entry into my new work and challenges."

With the help of Dr. Joseph Cammarosano as executive vice president and Dr. Paul Reiss, academic vice president and later executive vice president, Finlay worked to further the university's fiscal position. He worked with Wall Street financiers and other business executives to raise money, crediting them with "having taught a somewhat shy administration how to ask for money." One of the first changes enacted, according to former alumni director Ralph DeMayo, was to move the alumni office out of the Chrysler Building and onto the Lincoln Center campus, where it could be more effective.

Dr. Reiss agreed that they were not fundraisers. "One of the strengths, I have always felt, of the administration at Fordham during that period of time, and subsequently, was that the major administrative positions of Dean and Academic Vice President and other vice presidents were basically filled by people who had experience as faculty members at Fordham and who had close ties with members of the faculty. It, perhaps, was a more faculty-based administration than would be found at most universities."

In addition to the fiscal issues, Finlay had a number of agendas. One was to strengthen the teaching staff. Another was his determination that Fordham should provide career opportunities for women. He hired more female faculty members and placed some of them in positions of authority.

In a 1975 *New York Times* interview he said that earlier, when he had begun to realize obstacles that women were facing, he became incensed. "Why should talented women be shunted off to routine jobs when young men were being recruited for managerial training programs?" he said. "The waste of talent was bad enough. The affront to their qualities as human beings was simply infuriating."

Father Finlay repeatedly called on the faculty to get its act together and become more serious about teaching anything more than "gut courses."

After his presidency, he defended his position by comparing his own days as a Fordham student in the 40's (when Father Gannon also made faculty reforms). "There were brilliant intellects on campus, then as now, but I also recall a lot of inferior teaching whose tempo never changed from year to year. To those who sometimes remind me of 'those good old days,' I sometimes reply, 'well, number one, I remember them too so they can't be that old. And, second, they weren't so good because I experienced them. These are opinions that probably will not please everybody, but I am convinced that the quality of teaching at the Lincoln Center and Rose Hill campuses is now better and more constant than much of the instruction I received as an undergraduate."

To some extent the shortcomings of the faculty were due to age and evolution. The Jesuits who lit up classrooms during the 50's and 60's were quite old and nowhere near the stature of their earlier days as young men. Some, like Fr. George McMahon, earlier dean of the College and later moderator of the Fordham Band, were full of life and spirit, but others had seen better days.

I can remember Fr. Elbert Rushmore, who had been teaching at Fordham since 1950, old and hunched over, with a stunted gait, though still possessing a strong voice and the ability to gesture wildly. His theology lectures must have been fabulous in the past, but in the late 70's, they seemed automated and rote. There was certainly no give and take between teacher and student.

Perhaps some of the Jesuits were bitter and lost their spirit as the traditions they held dear were torn apart.

Lay teachers were adequate, but few were real scholars and still fewer were earning enough to be highly energized. They came to class in classic professors' clothing – mismatched pants and blazers with faded elbow patches – and assigned reading more than they lectured. Their classroom utterances were far from stimulating, with some exceptions, of course.

Richard Sheehan, class of 1988, is now a banker and part-time writer whose work largely revolves around financing independent films. He remembers a favorite professor, Dr. Tricia Curran from the communications department as one professor who stood out in his eyes.

"I don't know if there were any true scholars, but I had a great relationship with Dr. Curran, who headed the film program. She really encouraged me to write, and because there was only a Screenwriting I course when I was there, she created an advanced class over the summer just for me. I would write something and then send my work to her home in Connecticut. She even invited me to her house a few times to discuss the work and also to meet her in Old Greenwich for a movie; we saw *The Last Emperor* and sat for hours afterward discussing it. She was disappointed that I ended up in banking, and it is sad for me now that I am writing again, after all of these years, that she has passed away. It would have been great, if one of my scripts is ever produced, for Dr. Curran to have known about it."

Paul Phelan said "Panorama of World Religions" taught by Father O'Connell stood out for him. "Who would have known there were so many religions other than just Catholicism? My eyes were opened to so many other beliefs. If only I could have fit more electives into my schedule. The point is that Fordham opened me up to a world of differences."

Other respected professors of the era were reported to be Dr. Phyllis Zagano and Daniel Mack, both from the communications department and Professor John Entelis, political science chair and head of Middle East Studies, who remains at Fordham.

Change continued throughout the 70's and 80's.

Fordham College at Rose Hill merged with Thomas More College in 1974, making the whole university officially coeducational. That same year the College of Pharmacy closed due to declining enrollment.

Men and women were soon living in the same dorms, though in separate rooms. Alcohol and drugs were more prevalent. *The Ram*, previously censored, was now printing material from Planned Parenthood with information about birth control. A gay student organization was formed, FLAG (Fordham Lesbians and Gays). The group was not initially allowed to meet on campus, though after a bit of controversy, it was permitted to post meeting notices inside the university gates.

Father Robert Roth was made dean of Fordham College in 1974. His Values Program was supposed to emphasize the commitment to moral education, but many, even those from the old days like Professor John Olin, a history teacher, who arrived at Fordham in 1946 and mourned the old Jesuit-based classics, was opposed. He said, "The idea of having a certain segment of the curriculum or courses specifically devoted to values seemed to me totally ridiculous. Even more than that, all education, I thought, is a matter of values and you can't separate values as some specific topic that can be discussed one or two days a week in class. The educated man is a man with values." Father James Loughran succeeded Father Roth.

Unfortunately, crime arrived on campus and, especially, beyond its gates in the once quiet Belmont neighborhood.

Students and faculty were mugged. Walking down Fordham Road from the subway station at Jerome Avenue was something one thought twice about after dark, with good reason. The presence of IBI guards at every gate was quite a change from a few decades earlier when there was one campus police officer whose main job was said to be to keep neighborhood children off the grass.

In 1977, President Jimmy Carter visited the South Bronx to announce a plan to revive the area, making Charlotte Street famous. But that plan didn't really materialize for more than a decade afterward. The 1981 film, "Fort Apache: The Bronx," starring Paul Newman, was stunningly real in portraying the violence-prone borough during these years.

Enrollment, particularly at the College, started to decline. The university responded by adjusting admission requirements to allow students who might not have been at the top of their class to attend. According to Father Schroth, SAT scores were still required to be high, but high school grade point average standards were relaxed.

Father Quentin Lauer, the Prefect from Martyr's Court and a philosophy professor, remarked at the time that he could see the degradation of students. "In the 1950's, students were better equipped than they are now. I don't mean more intelligent, but more geared, especially linguistically, grammatically, to handle what they were studying. Just read the student newspaper, *The Ram*, and *The Monthly*, in the 40's and 50's and see how much better written they were than they are now. The grammar was better, the spelling was better, the thinking was more cogent. I think they were trained in high school better than they are now."

The physical plant, though still intrinsically beautiful, was a bit careworn. While the roses bloomed beautifully on the main road adjacent to Jack Coffey Field, many pathways were bare and the beautiful lawns were not as kept up as they are today. Classrooms were barren. Postcards and flyers would be posted on every bare wall and especially on the wooden posts surrounding Edward's Parade. Sadly, they would not be removed for months after the event they were promoting, unless rain washed them away.

Finlay put $24 million into rebuilding walls, repointing stone and brick, replacing ancient, unsafe electrical systems and transforming essentially sound and attractive, but outdated buildings into comfortable dormitories. He said, "Neither I nor my colleagues care particularly to be remembered as a 'caretaker administration,' but refurbishing, remodeling and better caretaking were overdue, and Rose Hill is much the better for it all."

Construction took place, but in the tradition of the era, the new structures lacked the beauty and grandeur of those erected decades earlier. First there was the $6 million Vincent T. Lombardi Memorial Center, a vast modern complex with an Olympic-sized swimming pool, an indoor track, tennis and basketball courts, and a fitness center to be used by all students and alumni, not just members of team sports. Interestingly, Vince Lombardi and Peter A. Carlesimo had started raising money for a new gym in the late 60's and early 70's, but Lombardi died before their vision could come to fruition. The plan morphed into the Lombardi Center after his death.

Another major new structure was the 13-story, elevator-equipped dormitory at 555 E 191ˢᵗ Street, now known as Walsh Hall, for former President Father Michael Walsh. Like so many in New York City during this era, it was and is cold and without artistic merit, closely resembling a public housing project. In fact, it was built facing the street as a condition of the loan Fordham received from New York City to build it. If Fordham had defaulted on the loan, the city would have converted it into – a housing project. This did not occur, of course, but the building's entrance remained confusingly off-campus, which also made it difficult to reach, until the university gate was finally extended.

Finlay purchased the Fordham Hospital site, 4.3 acres at the corner of Southern Boulevard and Fordham Road, for $400,000 from the city via auction. It would become a parking lot and later a multi-level parking structure.

Athletics suffered. Basketball coaches like P. J. Carlesimo and Digger Phelps came and went, as did Tom Penders. All went on to bigger and better venues. Carlesimo, son of the Fordham athletics director Peter A. Carlesimo (1968-78), went to Wagner College and then to the pros, including the Brooklyn Nets; Phelps went famously to Notre Dame and Penders to the University of Rhode Island. (P.J. Carlesimo was one of the 10 children his father, class of 1940, sent to Fordham.)

Radio station *WFUV*, where I spent most of my time from 1977 to 1981, was so ignored by the university that a dean or administrator was almost never seen within its walls on the third floor of Keating Hall, which might as well have been Siberia. There was a lone general manager hired by the university to watch over the station. The two in charge during my time, Frank A. Seitz and Don Barnett, rarely left their office. Seitz, a beloved staple at Fordham for years, was at the tail end of his career.

The absence of authority was good for the students, because unlike later years, the station was truly run by the students for the students, creating an amazing training ground for the many of us who landed real jobs in the media field in New York City, the nation's largest media market. We were disc jockeys, newscasters, content producers, schedulers, administrators and policy makers. We even had to raise money to keep the station going because the university's participation was limited to paying the station manager's salary, that of a chief engineer who maintained the transmitter, and footing the electric bill (hefty for a 24-hour, 50,000-watt radio station). Otherwise, as long as the Fordham games and Sunday Mass in the University Church were broadcast, there was seldom a peep from the president's office.

My classmates and I covered news at City Hall and at the national political conventions. We traveled to news and sporting events on the station's meager budget, generated by a fundraising marathon similar to those of public broadcasting, in large part supported by the wildly popular Irish music program, Ceol Na nGael. We did so with all the professionalism we could muster and with few antics, given the circumstances. It was beaten into us by our older peers that we were using the public airwaves and that we had to respect the FCC's rules and regulations or the station's license would be in peril.

(This point has been disputed in the press, most notably by Jim Dwyer of *The New York Times* who wrote about *WFUV* as a

virtual playground during those days [this in a story devoted to the late station manager Ralph Jennings, who ran the station when the university became involved again in the late 80's], but that can be chalked up to

The student-run days of WFUV. Clockwise from top right: Longtime General Manager Frank Seitz; Steve Hantzarides ('79); Ellen Webner ('79) and Dennis da Costa ('81) in the newsroom/music library; Joe McKenna ('80) and the author at the 1980 Democratic National Convention.

competition. Dwyer had been editor of *The Ram*, a long-time rival of *WFUV* for the journalism turf on campus.)

These were the years during which Denzel Washington was at Fordham living in 555. The Oscar-winning actor for "Training Day" and "Glory," the story of the Fordham-bred Civil War hero, Robert Shaw, grew up in Mount Vernon, New York. His

192

parents were divorced, but his mother was strict and made sure he stayed out of trouble in the neighborhood. A junior varsity

Photo: Fordham Archives

Denzel Washington graduated from Fordham in 1976 and received an honorary degree in 1991.

basketball player for two seasons (1972-74) under Coach P.J. Carlesimo, he was "just one of the guys" back then and even had a chipped front tooth, according to his teammates.

Darryl Brown, class of 1975 and a Boston Celtics draft pick, remembered Washington this way: "He played great defense, very quick. He had good hops; he was a slasher. He would drive hard to the basket. That's kind of the inner-city game. He didn't have the best of shots, but he had all of that tenacity. You didn't want him to guard you, let me put it that way. He knew where his strengths were; he would just get in your jock and he wouldn't let you go. That's the way he played. He was 6' 1" and a pretty decent ball handler, and he would go at the basket real hard."

Brown also remembers Washington as a solid person. "Denzel has never ever forgotten his boys. Every time he came to the city, a bunch of guys would get together and he'd hang. We'd go to his plays. I was working in radio for ABC, and every time we needed him to go on air with one of our national talents, he would always be there."

P.J. Carlesimo remembered Washington similarly. "My brothers or someone would say, 'Hey, did you see Denzel is doing a movie?' I remember that's what he wanted to do, but I'd be flat-out lying if I said, 'S---, I knew he was going to be great.'

He is stone 100 percent normal. He came with his boys to watch us practice with the Olympic team two Olympics ago. He's exactly the same, and I know that's a cliché. When he was doing some of the shows to promote 'Remember the Titans,' he said he modeled some of the character on his old college basketball coach. He was throwing me a little bone. Success has not changed him," said Carlesimo.

Indeed, Washington hadn't started out majoring in acting or even communications, but stumbled into the noted thespian Vaughn Deering's acting class, which eventually led to his transfer to the College at Lincoln Center for theater. Early reports of his performances were solid and his career took off rather quickly, starting with the NBC hit, "St. Elsewhere," in which he played a young doctor.

The backslide at Fordham continued through the late 70's into the 80s, concurrent with the national recession and New York City's toughest years yet. Father Finlay insisted that boosting the neighborhood was, at least in part, an answer to the troubles.

He said, "I was dismayed by the environmental and human aspects of decay outside the perimeter of Rose Hill, and I admit that one of my first acts to address a nearby problem had more vigor than intellect behind it. To city officials who would listen and to those who would not, I insisted more often than either group liked that a once-viable building across Fordham Road from the Third Avenue gate must be demolished to rid the area of a dangerous, disreputable eyesore. From that humble beginning we ventured into more important catalyst roles that stressed better neighborhood housing for the elderly and disabled, new entrepreneurial starts, neighborhood coalition formations to press for legitimate political action and response and similar actions."

Finlay moved to organize local business and clergy leaders who formed the Northwest Bronx Community Clergy Coalition.

They decided they had to take matters into their own hands, since the city wasn't going to do it.

Then they came up with the idea for Fordham Plaza. It would be a complex of office space, a department store, parking and smaller stores. They lobbied to get the city, the feds and private developers behind it, hoping the finished project would start to turn around the blight that was the Bronx at this time. The U.S. Postal Service owned the land across Fordham Road across from the campus, near Third Avenue. It took a lot to wrest the land out of that behemoth's hands.

Ultimately, Finlay threatened to move the whole university out of the Bronx, as NYU had done, saying he would relocate to Westchester County where Fordham already owned property at the Calder Estate, 114-acres then being used as an environmental research center. It was land that had been donated in 1967 for the Louis Calder Conservation and Ecology Study Center.

This was probably an empty threat since there was little chance Fordham would abandon its 150 years of buildings and identification with its storied location, but the tactic worked.

It took almost ten years, but ground was broken for a scaled down Fordham Plaza in 1984. The site now has offices, medical clinics, a bus station and even an Applebee's Restaurant. There was hope for the future, though the struggle was not over.

For students from the 70's and 80's, a number of whom were polled for this work, Fordham holds very special memories, even if it didn't produce a world-class education. Universally, graduates said they enjoyed their time at Fordham immensely, made lasting friendships, including friends and colleagues who formed a vast network, helping to shape careers.

"My parents, neither of whom went to college, were very proud that I graduated from there," said Richard Sheehan.

Certainly, there are thousands of very successful men and women who attended Fordham during these years, many of whom went on to great things.

Paul Phelan said, "I have to say that Fordham did its job. It prepared me for my future. The Career Placement Office assisted with finding me a job in New York City government, a job I still have today (there are many city agencies to work in). After 30 years, I am so happy to be able to say that in these turbulent times, with a family to support, I have never been without a job. I have a family, a wife and three children, a home, yes the American Dream. Fordham enriched my life with an opportunity to cultivate some of the best relationships, friends that remain today and friends I wouldn't have without my time at Fordham. Four-fifths of my bridal party was made up of Fordham alumni."

By 1983, Father Finlay was done. His replacement was the outgoing, but standoffish, Fr. Joseph Aloysius O'Hare, 53, the son of a New York City cop who, like Finlay, graduated from Regis High School and whose hometown was the Bronx, New York.

Chapter XII:
The Comeback Begins
Fordham in the Mid 80's and 90's

Prior to coming to Fordham in 1984, Father O'Hare had been editor in chief of *America* magazine, the national weekly journal of opinion published by the Jesuits in North America. He first joined its editorial staff in 1972, when he returned to the U.S. after teaching for a number of years at the Ateneo de Manila, a Jesuit university in the Philippines.

Though he was considered an outsider at first, Rev. J. Donald Monan, S.J., former president of Boston College (the finalist with Father Finlay for the Fordham presidency in 1972) said of O'Hare later on, "His early years as a Jesuit in Asia gave him a unique perspective on American culture, but his native New York gave him a directness, a maturity and a no-nonsense wisdom in leading that has reshaped the face of Fordham. "O'Hare had spent a few years as an adjunct instructor at Fordham in the 1970's and earned his Ph.D. there in philosophy, so he wasn't a total outsider."

Rev. Peter F. O'Brien, associate director of Campus Ministries at Lincoln Center described O'Hare as "always very sane," saying he was "no patsy at all – but he has no ax to grind, either."

Father O'Hare inherited a university in 1984, whose heyday was in the past. Though his predecessor had steered the ship through a storm, it would be the new guy's job to put the bloom back on Rose Hill. Like his immediate predecessor, he too would have a number of years to get the job done. He served for just less than 20 years making him the longest serving president in the institution's history.

Part of the challenge O'Hare faced had come about by circumstances beyond Fordham. There had been an evolution at the nation's 28 Jesuit colleges and a fear, now realized, that the lessening number of Jesuits (from 5,000 in the 60's to 1,000 in 1989) would mean an end to these colleges in their existing form, and especially that they would no longer be headed by Jesuits. Indeed, only eight of the 28 currently have lay presidents, including Georgetown, LeMoyne and St. Peter's, the longtime training ground for Fordham presidents.

A number of years after O'Hare took over, *The New York Times* said the Jesuit schools were once "all-male, all-Catholic institutions run by Jesuit priests in a style that alumni enjoy comparing to Marine boot camp." But, it said, "These colleges have passed a series of milestones that have included

Photo: Fordham University

Father O'Hare reached to the outside world. Pictured here with former Supreme Court Justice Sandra Day O'Connor.

coeducation, which in some colleges has resulted in a student body made up of mostly women; changes in the makeup of boards of trustees from priests to lay people and an ever-increasing number of non-Catholics among students and faculty members." For Fordham, check, check and check, though men still narrowly outnumber women.

O'Hare acknowledged at the time of his appointment, "The formal jurisdiction that exists is not the same kind of control (the Jesuits) had in the past. However, the Jesuit 'spirit' and 'tradition' still prevail on Fordham campuses."

Like Fordham, the other Jesuit schools at the time were suffering from small endowments, deteriorating physical plants and a lack of commitment from the alumni.

O'Hare became deeply involved with the inter-Jesuit university system and worked with it for solutions. He served as chairman of both the Association of Catholic Colleges and Universities (ACCU) and the Association of Jesuit Colleges and Universities (AJCU). In April 1989, he was part of the 18-member ACCU delegation to the Vatican Congress on Catholic Higher Education that was convened to develop materials for a Pontifical document on Catholic higher education.

The Rev. Paul S. Tipton, then president of the AJCU, told *The Times*, the colleges were "moving from using the word Jesuit to using the word Ignatian," a reference to St. Ignatius Loyola, the founder of the order in 1537.

"The point is that to describe an institution as Jesuit suggests it is run solely by the Jesuits, whereas Ignatian refers to the spirit of Jesuit education and to its emphasis on the link between the intellectual life and service to the community," said Tipton. "Put another way, St. Ignatius Loyola is no longer considered a role model as much as an inspirational force."

And that's where O'Hare received his cue. He felt that Fordham still had its moral compass and even though there was no longer the load of required philosophy and theology courses, there was still the spirit of merging the intellectual and moral aspects of life. Social justice and service learning were becoming part of the higher education vernacular that O'Hare would adopt. St. Ignatius would be referred to over and over again. Service learning was adopted as part of the curriculum.

He also charged his vice president for student affairs, Jay McGowan, with restoring order to the dorms and reducing the pursuit of drugs and alcohol. With the help of his successor, Father Joseph McShane, then dean of Fordham College, he expanded the curriculum to make it more robust, giving students a more global view of the world and of the multi-cultural society in which they lived. McShane's "baby" was the Matteo Ricci Society, which ushered students through the rigors of applying for Rhodes, Marshall and Fulbright scholarships, among others.

Soon Fordham became part of the real competition for these prizes.

Along these lines, the university became a late adopter to the idea of endowed chairs for research. Distinguished professors were also named. There was a Committee on Undergraduate Education that sought to beef up the enrollment strategy by incorporating the vice presidents and deans into the marketing and admissions process under the direction of Vice President for Enrollment Peter Stace.

O'Hare created the Laurence J. McGinley Chair in Religion and Society and, in 1987, appointed Rev. Avery Dulles, S.J., later Cardinal Dulles, to the position. Dulles was the son of President Eisenhower's secretary of state, John Foster Dulles and the nephew of Allen Dulles, a director of the CIA, who guided European espionage during World War II. Born a protestant, the Cardinal spent much time over the years at Fordham as a philosophy teacher in the 50's, as part of a number of summer school programs and also as a member of the Board of Trustees during Father Walsh's presidency.

The New York Times reported that when Pope John Paul II designated dozens of new cardinals in early 2001, the selection of Father Dulles was extraordinary. "Although his was an influential voice in American Catholicism, he was not even a bishop, let alone an archbishop.

"The appointment was widely seen as a reward for his loyalty to the pope, but also an acknowledgment of his work in keeping lines of communication open between the Vatican and Catholic dissenters in America. Cardinal Dulles considered it an honorary appointment. He was 82, two years past the age of voting with the other cardinals to elect a new pope," said the paper.

Dulles was staunchly against secularism and modernization. "Christianity," he said in a 1994 speech, "would dissolve itself if it allowed its revealed content, handed down in tradition, to be replaced by contemporary theories."

Dulles was so defensive that when the United States Conference of Catholic Bishops adopted a national policy barring any priest who had ever sexually abused a minor from ministerial duties, he said the policy ignored priests' rights of due process. According to *The Times*, he wrote:

"In their effort to protect children, to restore public confidence in the church as an institution and to protect the church from liability suits, the bishops opted for an extreme response," he said. He noted that the policy imposed a "one-size-fits-all" punishment, even if an offense was decades old and had not been repeated. "Such action seems to reflect an attitude of vindictiveness to which the church should not yield."

Despite what Dulles would have wanted, the Fordham student body became decidedly less Catholic, 74% in 2002, now between 50 and 75%, according to the university.

While O'Hare was one of Dulles' supporters, he was certainly more liberal, particularly where the Vatican was concerned. He was known to have resisted suggestions from Rome that the church exert more control over theology professors and what they taught.

O'Hare also had the right personality to be raising money as he desperately needed to do. With an outgoing personality given to that daunting task, he was often out on the town speaking, cheering for Fordham at games and attending events, sometimes serving as master of ceremonies and putting his outward gregariousness and sense of humor to use. He spent many years officiating at the annual Jesuit Mission Dinner held at the Waldorf Astoria.

In his inaugural address, O'Hare called for a greater engagement of the university in the life of New York City. In the tradition of Father Gannon, he took that on himself by serving on the boards of several institutions and on a number of city commissions. In 1988, Mayor Ed Koch appointed him founding chairman of a new agency that since has been hailed as a national model for campaign finance reform, the New York City Campaign Finance Board. He served until 2003.

In his official duties, O'Hare undertook a huge solicitation effort and revived the development office that had been in serious decline. An all-out effort was made to bring high profile/high net worth individuals to the Board of Trustees and to involve alumni in the university to foster their support.

Ultimately, he was able to raise

Photo: Fordham Athletics

The new Jack Coffey Field.

a great deal of money, to add approximately 1.1 million square feet of new academic and residential space and to oversee renovation of more than one million square feet of existing facilities.

O'Hare received funding for the incredible William D. Walsh Family Library in a $10 million grant from Mr. Walsh, class of 1951. Finally, Fordham would have the library for scholars and researchers it lacked for more than a century and a half. O'Hare made sure the building didn't look like a box; it was constructed to fit in with the other grand Gothic structures on campus. Inaugurated in 1997, the library on the Rose Hill campus is considered one of the most technologically advanced academic libraries in the country.

Jack Coffey Field was renovated in 1989. It now has seating for 7,000 and is a multi-purpose stadium, though it is best-known as home to the football team. With a reconstructed field, increased seating and indoor space, the stadium is a far cry from the facility first opened in 1930.

There was construction of additional residence halls, O'Hare Hall (formerly Sesquicentennial Hall) built in 1986 behind Spellman Hall, and Alumni Court added in 1987 near Queen's Court. O'Hare oversaw renovation of the landmarked University Church in 1990.

Father O'Hare merged the Lincoln Center and Rose Hill

O'Hare Hall

campuses to the extent that the curriculums would be shared and students could take courses at either location. In 1993, a 20-story residence hall was added to the Lincoln Center campus for 850 students. It is now named for the legendary Father George McMahon. In 1996, the campus's undergraduate college changed its name to "Fordham College at Lincoln Center," having been called "The Liberal Arts College" and later "The College at Lincoln Center."

To fill all the new residential space, O'Hare worked diligently to recruit students from beyond the New York metropolitan area, a move that was successful and continues to be so. Students now pile in from all over the country and the world. The student body is very different now than it was in the past, when it was made up almost exclusively of local individuals, the sons and daughters of working and middle class New York area parents.

The grounds started to look up again during the 90's. There was a real attempt to beautify Rose Hill especially, the result of which can easily be seen today by a stroll just about anywhere on campus.

One of O'Hare final acts was the 2000 takeover of Marymount College in Tarrytown, New York and the 2002 consolidation of Fordham and the independent women's college founded in 1907 by the Religious of the Sacred Heart of Mary. The merger did not last.

Fortunately, the Bronx began to return during his tenure, as did the city at large. Under Mayors Giuliani and Bloomberg, crime began a steady descent and graffiti disappeared from buildings and subway cars. A trip by a student to Yankee Stadium via the D train was no longer cause for trepidation. Parents could visit and take their children out to dinner on Arthur Avenue for a good Italian meal that was all of a sudden considered chic - and no longer a bargain. They could walk the few blocks from Fordham without putting their lives in peril.

Fordham felt the tragedy that struck the United States on September 11, 2001 with the loss of three students and 36 alumni. The students were Lloyd Brown, Patricia A. Cody and Christopher Dincuff, all graduate students. Among the Fordham graduates who perished was John M. Moran (Law School class of 1994), an attorney and New York City firefighter who had followed his father, uncle and brother to the FDNY. He was a battalion chief on Roosevelt Island who, like many of his fellow firefighters, rushed to the scene even though he was off duty. James Patrick (class of 1993), a bond broker at Cantor Fitzgerald, died seven weeks before his first child was born. Each of Fordham's two main campuses, Rose Hill and Lincoln Center, have a six-ton granite monument listing the names of those lost on 9/11. They were dedicated on September 11, 2002.

By the time Joe O'Hare was ready to transfer the reins in 2003, he had raised $150 million and grew the university's endowment to $271.6 million from $36.5 million, which was good for Fordham, but did not compare to that of Boston College at $1 billion. He increased enrollment, while also making admission requirements more stringent. SAT scores were higher than they had been in the 70's and 80's. Under O'Hare, Fordham's undergraduate applications nearly tripled, to 11,277 in 2002, from 4,064 in 1984.

When O'Hare stepped down, Paul B. Guenther, chair of the University's Board of Trustees, said, "During Father O'Hare's historic term as Fordham's 31st president, we have seen the physical transformation of both the Lincoln Center and Rose Hill campuses, the successful completion of the most ambitious fund-raising campaign in the University's history…and a three hundred percent increase in annual giving by alumni and friends. As a result Fordham stands on a much higher threshold for the next stage of its development."

Chapter XIII:
A University Embarks on its Third Century

And so the stage was set for Rev. Joseph Michael McShane, S.J., former dean of Fordham College and former president of Scranton University, who took over the Fordham presidency on July 1, 2003. His mission would be to continue to grow the university, to enhance its national reputation and to preserve its roots with fewer than 26 Jesuits actively involved in teaching and administration.

Father McShane, S.J., born in 1949, made his name as a theologian who spent many years as a professor of theology. Not an outsider by any means - his father and three brothers attended Fordham as undergraduates - he did his own undergraduate work at Boston College, perhaps a source of his goals for Fordham. He would set the bar even higher than it had been for Father O'Hare.

Like many of his predecessors, Father McShane grew up in New York City and graduated from Regis High School. At Boston College, he also earned a Master's degree in 1972. In 1977, he was ordained a priest and received Master of Divinity and Master of Sacred Theology degrees from the Jesuit School of Theology at Berkeley. His Ph.D. in the history of Christianity came from the University of Chicago in 1981.

Following in Father O'Hare's footsteps, McShane has become involved in the affairs of New York City. He was appointed to serve on the Commission on Metropolitan Transportation Authority (MTA) Financing in 2008.

In keeping with his credentials as a theologian, and with more outward references to Catholicism in his orations, Father McShane has stated on many occasions that Fordham's New York City location and its identity as a Jesuit institution are central to his vision for the university. He often states that he'd

like to make Fordham the country's preeminent Catholic
institution of higher learning, though the university remains
independent.

In his 10 years to date, he has made a great deal of progress
toward making Fordham bigger, brighter and more prestigious.

Only in recent years has Fordham become well known for its
promotion of research. The Carnegie Foundation for the
Advancement of Teaching currently classifies Fordham as a
doctoral university with high research activity. A significant
amount of the university's research is conducted in the natural
sciences, largely at the Louis Calder Center, a biological field
station operated by Fordham in Westchester. It consists of 114
forested acres, with a 10-acre lake and 19 buildings. The
structure houses laboratories and classrooms, offices for faculty
and administrators, a library and residences.

The university's William Spain Seismic Observatory is now a
data collection unit for the U.S. Geological Survey. In addition,
Fordham conducts research in cooperation with outside
organizations like the Bronx Scientific Research Consortium,
which includes the New York Botanical Garden, the Bronx Zoo,
Memorial Sloan-Kettering Cancer Center and Los Alamos
National Laboratory.

For undergraduates, it hosts an Undergraduate Research
Symposium every year and publishes an undergraduate research
journal in conjunction with the symposium, a major effort by
Dean of Fordham College Michael Latham. In addition, there
are research opportunities for undergraduates with such
organizations as the National Science Foundation, The Cloisters
and the American Museum of Natural History.

The Greek-lettered honors programs that eluded Father
Gannon back in the 1940's exist in greater numbers today.
Fordham has several honor societies on campus: Phi Beta Kappa
and Phi Kappa Phi, Alpha Sigma Nu (Jesuit), Beta Gamma Sigma
(business), Sigma Xi (scientific research), Psi Chi (psychology),

Sigma Delta Pi (Spanish), Omicron Delta Epsilon (economics), Lambda Pi Eta (communications) and Alpha Sigma Lambda (non-traditional students).

The Campion Institute is the university's office for academic fellowships and scholarships; it helped make Fordham one of the top producers of U.S. Fulbright students in 2012. Fordham also has one of the most extensive foreign study networks of any American university.

A short time after taking office, Father McShane and the Board of Trustees decided that the 2002 takeover of the financially struggling Marymount College was not working out. In 2005, it was decided that the university would close the Marymount campus by 2007 because enrollment was falling and finances had not improved. The last graduation took place in May of that year. At first it was thought the Fordham graduate programs would remain at that Westchester location, but in 2008, the university announced the sale of the campus for $27 million to EF Schools, a chain of private schools for language instruction. McShane called the decision a "painful" one and said the remaining programs would move to a new location in nearby West Harrison, New York.

Central to McShane's vision is the "cura personalis." He has said, "We have a great emphasis on care for the individual student; we have a great desire to introduce excellence and rigor into the classroom and every subject we teach; third, we believe that students have to be invited to wrestle with the great ethical issues of their time. We want them to be bothered by the realization that they don't know everything and bothered by injustice."

To that end, McShane expanded the Dorothy Day Center for Service and Justice, responsible for overseeing Fordham's various community service and humanitarian initiatives. Grounded in the Jesuit principle of homines pro aliis (men and women for others), the center organizes projects in such areas as poverty, hunger, education and disaster relief. As a result of Dorothy Day's efforts, the students performed approximately one million hours of service in 2011, ranking it sixth in the country in terms of community outreach.

As the university approaches its 175th anniversary in 2016, McShane in 2006 unveiled a plan to enhance the reputation and quality of education at Fordham. Known as the Toward 2016 Integrated Strategic Plan, to be implemented in time for the next major jubilee, it will entail a $500 million investment to enhance the university's profile, increase faculty research, make capital improvements to Rose Hill and Lincoln Center, increase the competitiveness of varsity sports and grow the university's endowment.

McShane has identified four key components of the plan:

- To advance the culture of scholarship, teaching, research and service for faculty by investing in endowed chairs and faculty development to enhance recruitment and retention and secure world-class stature for university professors.
- To develop graduate and professional programs that can win distinctive excellence, national prominence and external support, as well as enhance the graduate and professional learning environment.
- To develop and sustain an undergraduate culture of learning and living that will be recognized for distinctive excellence and achieve national prominence.
- To generate and sustain the funding necessary to support investments in physical resources and the university endowment, and to fuel growth in annual giving.

At Rose Hill, already completed portions of the 2016 plan include two new undergraduate residence halls (2010), renovation of Hughes Hall, now home to the Gabelli School of Business (2011) and a new exercise facility (2012). Still to come are the reorganization of dining facilities, renovation of various residential and science facilities, new offices for faculty and administrators, a new student union, a new science building and the renovation of Collins Auditorium.

At Lincoln Center, the strategy, approved by the New York City Council in 2009, involves razing several buildings on the eight-acre campus to make room for a new School of Law, an expanded library, student housing, a student activities center and parking. The plan will add 1.5 million square feet to the current campus.

Father McShane, known for being accessible to students, faculty and alumni – he answers every email sent to him personally – has made good on many of his promises. The university continues to grow with four undergraduate schools: Fordham College at Rose Hill (Fordham College), 1841; the Gabelli School of Business, 1920; the School of Professional and Continuing Studies, 1944; Fordham College at Lincoln Center, 1968; and six additional graduate schools, the School of Law, 1905; Graduate School of Arts and Sciences, 1916; Graduate School of Education, 1916; Graduate School of Social Service, 1916; Joseph M. Martino Graduate School of Business Administration, 1969, and the Graduate School of Religion and Religious Education, 1969.

The university's library system, once criticized as subpar for a university of its size, is considered top notch. In addition to holding more than two million volumes, the library also subscribes to 439,000 online books. The university is a government depository and the library holds 380,000 hard copy documents and 109,000 online government documents. The William D. Walsh Library at Rose Hill has the university archives and special collections, along with a separate science library. There is also the Quinn Library at Fordham Lincoln

Center and the Westchester Library at the West Harrison campus.

Fordham maintains several special collections that are housed in various museums and galleries on campus. The Fordham Museum of Greek, Etruscan, and Roman Art is located at Rose Hill and contains more than 200 artifacts from classical antiquity. Another gift from William D. Walsh, it is the largest collection of its kind in the New York metropolitan area. In addition, the university maintains an extensive art collection, housed at exhibition spaces at Rose Hill and Lincoln Center and in galleries around New York City. The collection will eventually be on permanent display at the Fordham University Art Gallery, currently under construction at Lincoln Center.

Photo: Pamela O'Sullivan
Bono at Fordham in March 2009.

As of this writing, there are 15,189 students in 10 schools at Fordham, including 8,427 undergraduates. A good many, 4,096, live in university housing. There are 6,762 graduate and professional students. The graduation rate is 78%, well above the national average of 56%. There are slightly more men than women accepted each year.

Fordham University's average SAT scores fall in the low to mid 600s in all three categories: verbal, math and writing.

Ninety-four percent of all faculty members hold a Ph.D. or the highest degree they can attain in their field. The undergraduate student to faculty ratio is 14:1 and the average class has 23 students. There are 20 Jesuits currently teaching at Fordham and six working in administrative positions.

The school's annual budget is nearly $500 million and its endowment is $510.8 million. In 2013, Fordham was ranked 58th by *U.S. News & World Report* among America's Best Colleges in the category of national universities.

Fordham sponsors 23 men's and women's varsity sports teams. The Fordham Rams are members of NCAA Division I and compete in the Atlantic 10 Conference in baseball, basketball, cross country, diving, golf, rowing, soccer, softball, squash, swimming, tennis, indoor and outdoor track, volleyball and water polo; and in the Patriot League (Division I-AA) for football.

The entrance to the Administration Building.

Perhaps a throwback to the university's earliest times, the school now has a number of residential colleges where students live and learn as a group, dining together and participating in extracurricular activities that support the mission of their community. Housed in O'Hare Hall, which has an architectural design to support the concept, it is a particularly nurturing community with 13 staff members and two Jesuits in residence.

The Integrated Learning Community for Ignatian Leadership and Civic Service is for second and third year students from Fordham College at Rose Hill and the Gabelli School of Business. It stresses an interdisciplinary connection on such topics as international affairs, government policy, public relations, ethical business practices and effective leadership. Its

212

goal is to inspire well-rounded, confident students who will affect change at Fordham University and in the world.

The Integrated Learning Community – Global Business combines business and ethics education to enhance a student's cultural intelligence. There is a focus on the integration of academic excellence, residential activities and service aimed at developing international business skills.

There is even Wellness Housing where each resident signs an agreement promising to live in an alcohol, drug and tobacco free environment. This dorm section offers a wide range of social, educational, physical and spiritual programs.

If you have a Fordham BA or BS, you'll be happy to know you're one of 78,000 people with that distinction; those with advanced degrees number 74,000. If you're considering sending your child to Fordham, you'll be interested, if not happy, to know that tuition is $57,106 per year, including room and board. Fordham is the most expensive Catholic college in the nation and now costs more than Harvard and Princeton.

Presidents of the United States no longer visit Fordham, possibly attributable to New York's status as solidly Democrat in its voting – the state is no longer a stomping ground for any national politicians. Though it continues to turn out leaders in society, including the current Governor of New York State, Andrew Cuomo, class of 1979, and the head of the CIA, John Brennan, class of 1977, the university continues its comeback. Occasionally, there are moments of fame, as when the mega-star Bono of U-2 gave a concert on campus as part of a national broadcast by ABC. Commencement speakers tend to be broadcasters and business leaders – in 2013 it was the NBC foreign correspondent Richard Engel – and there are few flashes of national prominence.

Almost a century and three-quarters after its founding, Fordham is a bit more crowded with people and with structures, but it also remains as bucolic as the day Archbishop Hughes held his birthday/dedication back in June 1841. The main Fordham campus at Rose Hill, featured in *MSNBC's* 2008 edition of "America's Prettiest College Campuses," continues to be distinguished by the old elm trees first written about in the 1800's. It still has the greatest examples of collegiate Gothic architecture, expansive lawns, ivy-covered buildings and cobblestone streets in the U.S. It would be hard to improve on the standards assigned to maintenance and grounds keeping. It is nearly perfect.

Surely more important is that the Fordham spirit remains.

Will Zawacki, 21, is one of Fordham's newest graduates, from the class of 2013, and he already has a job. His grandfather was a Fordham alumnus. A graduate of the Gabelli School of Business, he's working at Footlocker as a merchandise planner where he analyzes sales trends. Will already credits Fordham with helping his career via various internships he did as a student, and like his older counterparts, thanks the university's embracing spirit for providing a nurturing experience during his four years.

Zawacki recognizes, even now, that he has made friends for life and credits members of the faculty for always being available and ready to help. Specifically, he said, his business communications professor, Kate Combellick, threw away the textbooks and offered Will and his classmates the opportunity to learn about business as they were learning about themselves – what they wanted to do with their lives, what their strengths and weaknesses were. He also applauds the community service opportunities at Fordham for providing an outlet to help others and to help him meet other Fordham students.

Finally, he thought Father McShane was a leader among leaders, remarking at how captivating he and other students found the president's talks and lectures. He said whenever he saw McShane near a microphone he perked up, knowing he was about to hear something inspirational. McShane touched him personally by being there with prayers when a young friend was dying of cancer.

After 172 years, it can be said that Archbishop Hughes' dream of providing a world-class institution of higher education for Catholic men in and around New York City has been realized – and then some. Since 1841 and the implementation of its first curriculum, Fordham has continuously upheld the importance of a solid core curriculum to provide all students with a strong liberal arts education. The liberal arts education at Fordham College provides students with the knowledge, resources and background to enter the world with the ability to successfully contribute to the various fields of education, law, social service, religion, business and the arts. Hail men (and women) of Fordham, Hail!

Acknowledgements

A number of wonderful people have assisted in the collection of research for this book. Starting at Fordham, I owe a big debt of gratitude to the Director of Archives, Patrice Kane, and to her associate, Vivian Shen, who procured photographs and checked facts. Also at the university, Catherine Spencer and Ryan Stellabotte of the public affairs office, Todd Melnick at the law school and Scott Kwiatkowski in athletics, all supplied photographs.

Fordham College Dean Michael Latham was extremely obliging in making introductions to others on campus. Historian Dr. Allan Gilbert was more than kind in agreeing to read the manuscript to make sure the details added up. He also shared the pre-publication version of a book he is writing with Dr. Roger Wines on the archeological dig the two conducted at Fordham from 1985 to 2002, which was very kind – and helpful.

Many former professors and students at Fordham (spanning 1946 to 2013) were generous with their time by granting interviews and contributing reflections: Frank Corbin, Rosemary Flannery, Gerri Paré, Jack Phelan, Paul Phelan, my great friend, Richard Sheehan and William Zawacki, referred by Kathleen Reilly, a proud Fordham mom and my close friend from our days as first graders.

Those on the board of the Fordham College Alumni Association have had the greatest ideas. Norma Vavolizza pointed me to a number of friends and colleagues with information, as did Paul Gerken and Kat McBride. Norma and Ann McNulty read early drafts.

There were a number of people who were unknown to me before the start of this process who, nonetheless, offered terrific stories, information and photographs. Among them were members of the family of Charles Curtin, especially Mary Barbara

216

Huber. Peter Riva answered my questions and put me in touch with his mother, Maria Riva, the daughter of Marlene Dietrich.

I couldn't have gotten this project started or finished without my colleagues at E-Lit Books – the wonderful Fran Black and Jenn Mishler.

My family is behind everything I do because they help me get through life and they listen to my stories, especially those revolving around Fordham. Thank you Jennifer Marrone Bonislawski and Stephanie Marrone. Finally, I don't know where I would be without the greatest husband in the world, Mike Marrone.

Fordham Presidents

Archdiocese

1841-1843	Fr. John McCloskey
1843-1844	Fr. John Harley
1844-1846	Fr. James Roosevelt Bayley

Society of Jesus

1846-1851	Fr. Augustus J. Thébaud, S.J.
1851-1854	Fr. John Larkin, S.J.
1854-1859	Fr. Remigius I. Tellier, S.J.
1859-1863	Fr. Augustus J. Thébaud, S.J.
1863-1865	Fr. Edward Doucet, S.J.
1865-1868	Fr. William Moylan, S.J.
1868-1874	Fr. Joseph Shea, S.J.
1874-1882	Fr. F. William Gockeln, S.J.
1882-1885	Fr. Patrick Dealy, S.J.
1885-1888	Fr. Thomas J. Campbell, S.J.
1888-1891	Fr. John Scully, S.J.
1891-1896	Fr. Thomas Gannon, S.J.
1896-1900	Fr. Thomas J. Campbell, S.J.
1900-1904	Fr. John A. Petit, S.J.
1904-1906	Fr. John J. Collins, S.J.
1906-1911	Fr. Daniel J. Quinn, S.J.
1911-1915	Fr. Thomas J. McCluskey, S.J.
1915-1919	Fr. Joseph A. Mulry, S.J.
1919-1924	Fr. Edward P. Tivnan, S.J.
1924-1930	Fr. William J. Duane, S.J.
1930-1936	Fr. Aloysius J. Hogan, S.J.
1936-1949	Fr. Robert I. Gannon, S.J.
1949-1963	Fr. Laurence J. McGinley, S.J.

1963-1965	Fr. Vincent T. O'Keefe, S.J.
1965-1969	Fr. Leo P. McLaughlin, S.J.
1969-1972	Fr. Michael P. Walsh, S.J.
1972-1983	Fr. James C. Finlay, S.J.
1984-2003	Fr. Joseph A. O'Hare, S.J.
2003-	Fr. Joseph M. McShane, S.J.

Notable Fordham Alumni

- Geraldine Ferraro, first female U.S. vice presidential candidate from a major political party
- Joseph Cao, Jerrold Nadler, Bill Pascrell, and Adam Smith; U.S. Congressmen
- Andrew Cuomo, governor of New York State, U.S. Secretary of Housing and Urban Development (1997-2001)
- John N. Mitchell, U.S. Attorney General (1969-1972)
- William J. Casey, U.S. Director of Central Intelligence (1981-1987)
- John O. Brennan, U.S. Director of Central Intelligence
- G. Gordon Liddy, Chief Operative, White House Plumbers
- Hage Geingob, first prime minister of Namibia
- Francis Spellman, Cardinal of the Roman Catholic Church (1946-1967)
- E. Gerald Corrigan, chairman of Goldman Sachs Bank USA, president of the Federal Reserve Bank of New York (1985-1993)
- Lorenzo Mendoza, CEO of Empresas Polar
- Anne M. Mulcahy, chairwoman and CEO of Xerox (2001-2009), named one of the "50 Most Powerful Women in Business" in 2006
- Don Valentine, founder of Sequoia Capital
- Wellington Mara, owner of the New York Giants NFL franchise (1959-2005)
- Steve Bellán, the first Latin American to play Major League Baseball
- Peter A. Carlesimo, Executive Director of the National Invitational Tournament (1978-1988)
- John Mulcahy, Olympic gold and silver medalist

- John Skelton, quarterback of the Arizona Cardinals NFL franchise
- Denzel Washington, two-time Oscar and three-time Golden Globe-winning actor
- Alan Alda, six-time Emmy and six-time Golden Globe-winning actor
- Patricia Clarkson, Emmy-winning and Oscar-nominated actress
- Lana Del Rey, Brit Award-winning singer-songwriter
- Amanda Hearst, socialite and heiress to the William Randolph Hearst fortune
- Charles Osgood, three-time Emmy and two-time Peabody Award-winning journalist
- Michael Kay, television announcer for the New York Yankees
- Jim Dwyer, two-time Pulitzer Prize-winning journalist
- Mary Higgins Clark, bestselling novelist
- Virginia O'Hanlon, whose 1897 letter to *The New York Sun* prompted the famous reply, "Yes, Virginia, there is a Santa Claus"
- William J. McGill, president of Columbia University (1970-1980)
- Timothy S. Healy, president of Georgetown University (1976-1989)
- John Sexton, president of New York University
- George Coyne, director of the Vatican Observatory (1978-2006)

Notable Fordham Faculty

- Joseph Abboud, fashion designer
- Bruce Andrews, political scientist and poet
- Hilaire Belloc (fl. 1937), writer and historian
- Doron Ben-Atar, historian and playwright
- Daniel Berrigan, peace activist and poet
- Mary Bly, bestselling novelist, also known as "Eloisa James"
- Joseph Campbell (fl. 1925-1939), Irish poet and lyricist
- John M. Culkin (fl. 1964-1969), media scholar
- Cardinal Avery Dulles (fl. 1988-2008), Christian theologian
- Victor Francis Hess (fl. 1938-1958), Nobel laureate in physics
- William T. Hogan (fl. 1950-2002), economist, known as the "steel priest"
- Elizabeth Johnson, Christian theologian and feminist
- Carl Jung (fl. 1912), psychologist
- Joseph Koterski, philosopher
- Paul Levinson, writer
- Mark S. Massa, Christian theologian
- John James Maximilian Oertel (fl. 1841-1846), German scholar and journalist
- Marshall McLuhan (fl. 1967-1968), philosopher and communications scholar.
- Margaret Mead (fl. 1968-1970), cultural anthropologist
- William O'Malley, Christian theologian, actor in and technical advisor for The Exorcist
- Mark D. Naison, American social historian and political activist
- Diana Villiers Negroponte, legal scholar
- Willie Perdomo, poet and writer

- Phylicia Rashad (fl. 2011-2012), Tony Award-winning actress
- Asif Siddiqi, aerospace historian
- Werner Stark (fl. 1963-1975), sociologist and economist
- Dietrich von Hildebrand (fl. 1940-1960), philosopher and Christian theologian

Footnotes

Introduction

Passage	Source
"Fordham College...the spot."	Thomas Gaffney Taaffe. *A History of St. John's College, Fordham, N.Y.* London, England: The Catholic Publication Society Co., 1891, p2-25 (Taaffe) Thomas C. Hennessey, S.J. *Fordham The Early Years,* New York: Fordham University Press, 1998

Chapter I

Passage	Source
"In 1840...August 29, 1839."	Taaffe p30-48 A.S. Gilbert & Roger Wines. *In Digging The Bronx: Recent Archaeology in the Borough (Seventeen Years of Excavations at Rose Hill Manor, Fordham University),* Bronx, New York: The Bronx County Historical Society, in prep (edited by A.S. Gilbert.), p42-47 (Gilbert/Wines)
"Hughes...political regeneration."	John Hassard. *Life of the Most Reverend John Hughes.* New York, D. Appleton & Company, 1866 Edward Dunigan. Series: Pamphlets in American History. Catholicism and anti-Catholicism, John Hughes, 1848
"Surly and...like cross."	William Stern. *City Journal: How Dagger John Saved New York's Irish,* Spring 1997

"Hughes was quoted…put me down."	Orestes Brownston. *Brownston's Quarterly Review, Vol. 2,* p84, New York, 1874
"When he…schools and hospitals."	Catholic Encyclopedia
"The Archbishop…flagrant kind."	Taaffe, p43-44
"Though the society…Catholic Churches."	William Stern. *City Journal: How Dagger John Saved New York's Irish,* Spring 1997
"Hughes fought…a second Moscow."	Edward Wakin. *Enter the Irish-American:* Bloomington, IN, iUniverse, 2002
"The Know-Nothing…I Know Nothing."	Wikipedia.org
"St. John's College…north of Georgetown."	Fordham.edu
"To procure…percent interest."	Taaffe, p51
"Whether by luck…original plan."	Hennessey, p140
"Hughes chose…Edward's Parade."	Taaffe, p51-52
"The only women…group of boys."	Gilbert/Wines, p50
"St. John's first…Revolutionary War."	Taaffe, p52
"but the only…through the area."	Gilbert/Wines, p53
"The wooden structure…central portion."	Taaffe, p52
"As built…and offices."	Hennessey, p142-144
"It was here…other prelates."	Taaffe, p52
"Beyond the buildings…ice production."	Hennessey, p144-148
"Our Lady of Mercy…at Fordham."	Fordham.edu

"By 1846...outstanding structures."

Taaffe, p52

Gilbert/Wines, p47

"Over the first...substantial tower."

Hennessey, p146

"In the 1940's...the old one."

Robert I. Gannon, S.J. *Up to the Present: The Story of Fordham,* Garden City, N.Y., Doubleday & Co., 1967, p238-239 (Gannon)

"After World War II...St. John's Hall."

Fordham.edu

"The second building...called Queens Court."

Taaffe, p58-59

"Other, smaller...could wash."

Hennessey, 144

"Hughes knew what...Dramatist and poet."

Robert R. Rusk. *The Doctrines of the Great Educators, Revised:* New York, Macmillan, 1957.

"In June 1846...of it permanently."

Taaffe, p69

Gannon, p37

Raymond A. Schroth, S.J. *Fordham: A History and Memoir, Revised:* New York, Fordham University Press, 2008. (Schroth)

"Even though Hughes...smooth things over."

Gannon, p50-52

"Born in Nantes...life in France."

Wikipedia.org

"During Father Thébaud's...his name."

Gannon, p42

"In addition...1861"

Schroth, p41

"It was in 1847...disputed."

Gannon, p18

"I knew him well...instinct."

The Fordham Monthly, "Some Reminiscences," June 1891

"On June 15, 1847... you contract."

New York Herald, June 16, 1847

"Father Larkin…at Fordham."	Schroth, p38-42
"No Man…Greek God."	Taaffe, 87
"First, a uniform…of the pupil."	Robert R. Rusk. *The Doctrines of the Great Educators, Revised:* New York, Macmillan, 1957.
"While Larkin… that year."	Taaffe, p87-89
"One of the few…33-11."	Gannon, p56-57
"One of the team's… in Cuba."	*Fordham Magazine*, Winter 2009
"Father Tellier…June."	Taaffe, p95
"And was known…Egerton Wilks."	Gannon, p55-56
"The pre-Civil War…intertwined."	Taaffe, p98
"A single teacher…also competitive."	Hennessey, p155
"Father Tellier…which remain."	Taaffe, p98
"Among the first…Jesuit priests."	Taaffe, p106-107
"As noted…and schools."	Thomas F. Meehan. *John Rose Greene Hassard:* New York, Robert Appleton Company, 1913
"One of the most…New York audience."	*New York Tribune*, February 28, 1860

Chapter II

Passage	Source
"Unlike Georgetown…vice versa."	Georgetown.edu
"There was no…Jefferson Davis."	Augustus J. Thébaud. *Forty Years in the United States of America:* United States Catholic Historical Society, 1904, p90

"Archbishop Hughes...for the Union."

John Gjerde. *Catholicism and the Shaping of Nineteenth Century America:* Cambridge University Press, 2011, p253
Fordham Magazine, Winter 2009

"According to Father...southern states."

Gannon, p60-61

"Among those...Bellinger."
"Union General Martin...in Manhattan."

Pinckneyfamily.com/history-4.html
Catholic Encyclopedia
Civil War Medal of Honor Recipients, United States Army Center of Military History, June 16, 2007

"From General McMahon's...Army of the Potomac."

The New York Times, "Gen. Martin T. McMahon Dies of Pneumonia," April 22, 1906, p9

"Another Fordham war hero...a body-guard he has."

Peter Burchard. *One Gallant Rush:* New York, St. Martin's Press, 1965
Henry Cabot Lodge, Theodore Roosevelt. *Hero Tales from American History:* The Minerva Group, Inc., Jun 1, 2001, p109
Lorien Foote. *Seeking the One Great Remedy: Francis George Shaw and Nineteenth-Century Reform:* Ohio University Press, 2003, p119
Boston City Council, Exercises at the Dedication of the Monument to Colonel Robert Gould Shaw, Boston Municipal Printing Office, May 31, 1897

"Gen. James Rowan...Irish Rifles."

James E. Honans. *The Cyclopaedia of American Biography:* 1900
The New York Times, "Gen. Jas. R. O'Beirne Dies in 77th Year," February 18, 1917
Damian Shiels. *The Irish in the American Civil War.* History Press Limited, 2013
Fordham College Monthly, Vol. 34, Fordham University, 1915

Passage	Source
"Among the even…St. John's students."	Schroth, p75
"Frederick Goggins…of the gulf."	*Woodstock Letters*, *"Letters from a Chaplain in the War of 1861,"* XVIII, No. 1, 1889, p23
"Another drummer boy…1872."	*Fordham Alumni Magazine*, *"Morgan J. O'Brien, '72,"* March 1932, p10
"One, Father Thomas…Gaffney's book."	Taaffe, p90
"Of Father Nash…officers."	Schroth, p75
"Father Peter Tissot…in time."	*Fordham Monthly*, *"A Year with the Army of the Potomac: Diary of the Rev. Father Tissot, S.J., Military Chaplain"*
"Father Doucet was…to Europe."	Taaffe, p100
"Father Doucet's…50th anniversary."	Taaffe, p103

Chapter III

Passage	Source
"In the early 1850's…still $30."	Course Catalogue, St. John's College 1862-1871
"The students continued…they were."	Consultor's Record Book, April 1, 1867, AFU
BOX	Rules and Customs Book, St. John's College, circa 1865
"A farm…at the time."	Hennessey, p147
"The ram…year 1841."	Fordham.edu
"By 1868…was just 166."	Course Catalogue, St. John's College 1862-1871
"Shea…arrived in 1883"	Taaffe, p104-107
	Gannon, p76
"Father Shea…ceiling."	Schroth, p96

Notable students of….among men."   Taaffe, p107

"These years…in those years."   Catholic Encyclopedia
"Former St. John's…institutional peers."   Augustus J. Thébaud. *Forty Years in the United States of America: 1839-1885:* U.S. Catholic Historical Society, 1904

"Notable growth…the Vatican."   Schroth, p90
"Father Robert Gannon…outside the gate."   Gannon, p78

"Catholicism…City of New York."   Timothy P. Slattery. *Loyola and Montreal:* Montreal, Palm Publishers, 1962

"One of the first…elect officers."   *Fordham Monthly*, October 9, 1882
"In 1883…decades later."   Gannon, p83
"Dealy also set…building to building."   Taaffe, p112-113

"In April 1879…a college administrator."   Schroth, p104
Thomas C. Hennessey, S.J. *Fordham The Early Years:* New York, Fordham University Press, 1998

"From 1885 to…national cemetery."   Gannon, p82
Wikipedia.org
"The college…God We Trust."   Gannon, p88
"The first incandescent…today's Dealy."   Taaffe, p116

"The day…school-wide."   Fordham.edu
"The New York Times…of society."   *The New York Times, "St. John's Half Century: An Interesting Anniversary at the Fordham College,"* June 25, 1891

"It was…gave speeches."   *Fordham Monthly*, March 1893
"An early graduate…later on."   *The New York Times, "Ex-Senator Dead, Edward J. Murphy, Jr.,"* August 4, 1911

"As the Spanish…continuing issue."   Gannon, p115-117

Chapter IV

Passage	Source
"A number of well-known."	Schroth, p148
"The extension...north of Fordham."	Wikipedia.org
"The college...Fordham Medical School."	Gannon, p119
"In 1902...60-yard invitational."	Gannon, p121
"Little old...lack of sleep."	Fordham.edu
"While Father Collins....deducted annually."	Gannon, p128-129
"Fordham Law...Exam passed."	Fordham.edu
	Gannon, p127
"The Fordham University...in 1931."	Fordham.edu
"Father Quinn's...law school."	Gannon, p133
"The College...and pedagogy (education)."	Fordham.edu
BOX	Fordham.edu
"The story of...coming years."	Gannon, p134-138
	Schroth, p123-128
	New York Sun, September 17, 1912
	Wikipedia.org
	Fordham Magazine, Winter 2009
"The Rev. Joseph...to the Bronx."	*The New York Times*, *"The Rev. Joseph A. Mulry, Noted Jesuit Dies,"* September 1, 1921
"Father Mulry said...round the world."	Gannon, p144-15
"Almost simultaneously...spinal injury."	Wikipedia.org

"At the jubilee...favorite teacher."	*The New York Times, "Fordham Turns Out Its Largest Class,"* June 15, 1916
"On the athletic...central cross."	*Woodstock Letters,* 1916
"The Monthly...the Almighty."	*Fordham Monthly,* April 1917
"Major Robert...War Cross."	Gannon, p150-151
"As detailed...war wounded."	*The Maroon,* 1920
	Interviews with members of the Curtin family
"The Woodstock Letters...from Fordham."	*Woodstock Letters*
"By the time...and services."	Schroth, p136
"That summer...football team."	Gannon, p152-153
"According to the book...$3.8 billion."	Robert J. Kaczorowski. *Fordham University School of Law: A History*: New York, Fordham University Press, 2012
"In the end...Army."	Gannon, p155
"Thirty-six students...lives overseas."	Schroth, p136
"The war, tragically...1921."	*Fordham Monthly, "The Life of Father Mulry,"* October 1921
"In its obituary...his successor."	*The New York Times, "The Rev. Joseph A. Mulry, Noted Jesuit Dies,"* September 1, 1921
"A footnote...the hierarchy."	Fordham Law School Faculty Minutes Book, Advisability of Admitting Women, 1918
"At long last...and lawyers."	*The Ram,* February 11, 1938, p3
"The IRT...in the U.S."	Wikipedia.org
"Another high note...I wish."	Schroth, p137
	Sport Magazine, 1949

Chapter V

Passage	Source
"By 1920…was raised"	Gannon, p166
BOX	Fordham.edu
"At the campus…on hand."	Gannon, p163-164
"The present…Weigel."	Fordham.edu
"Even though…collegiate championship."	Fordham.edu
"One of Father…football team."	Gannon, 167-170
"According to…gets none."	*Fordham Monthly*, February 1918, p88
"A Fordham…athletic activities."	Gannon, p171
"I am also…only harm."	Father Tivnan letter, June 7, 1920
"The situation today…bills promptly."	Father Tivnan letter, November 22, 1921
"In another…clean years."	Father Tivnan letter, 1924
"Team sports…influence of Jack."	Wikipedia.org Society for American Baseball Research, Maurice Bouchard, SABR.org
"In 1924…previous number."	Gannon, p173
"This magnificent…of biologists."	*Fordham Monthly*, 1927
"A biology student…to him."	*As I Remember Fordham: Selections from the Sesquicentennial Oral History Project:* New York, Fordham University Press, 1991, Dr. James Forbes (Oral History)
"Another student…you in class?"	Oral History, Dr. John Collins
"In concert with…his domain."	Oral History, George A. Brooks
"The 1932 kidnapping…*Jafsie Tells All*."	University of Missouri- Kansas City School of Law, http://law2.umkc.edu/faculty/

	projects/ftrials/Hauptmann/condon.html
"During Father Duane's...settlement."	Gannon, p174
"The next year...Franklin Delano Roosevelt."	Oral History, Tom Quinn
"Father Duane...signed up."	Gannon, p179
"It is no...before them."	*Fordham Monthly*, October 1926

Chapter VI

Passage	**Source**
"But academics...at the time."	Philip Gleason. *Contending with Modernity: Catholic Higher Education in the 20th Century:* Oxford University Press, 1995
"We refuse...a winner."	Gannon, p198
	Schroth, p144
	Fordham.edu
	Woodstock Letters
"Hogan's main...losing money."	Schroth, p145
"The football team...to 1941."	Fordham.edu
	ESPN, *"Captain of Fordham's 'Seven Blocks of Granite' Dies,"* December 29, 2005
	Oral History, John Canella
	Wikipedia.org
"Lombardi...all the time."	David Maraniss. *When Pride Still Mattered*, New York, Simon & Schuster, 2010
"At Fordham...a wop."	Schroth, p148
"There is no doubt...the character."	Vincelombardi.com

"Edward P. Gilleran…enough   Oral History, Edward P. Gilleran, Jr.
for us."

Chapter VII

Passage	Source
"When Father Robert…Fordham hierarchy."	Gannon, p207-209
"When Gannon…Phi Beta Kappa."	Philip Gleason. *Contending with Modernity: Catholic Higher Education in the 20th Century:* Oxford University Press, 1995
"Gannon decided…European historian."	Schroth, p159-160 Fordham.edu
"To continue…for the university."	Gannon, p210
"After many years…in that era."	Gannon, p227
"As alluded to…Doctor of the Church."	Fordham.edu
"Additionally, Gannon…Pax Romana Congress."	*Gannon, p230* *Fordham.edu* *John Cooney.* The Life and Times of Francis Cardinal Spellman: *New York, New York Times Books, 1984* The New York Times, "Guileless and Machiavellian: The American Pope," *October 28, 1984* *Wikipedia.org*
"Also in 1940…a cup of tea."	Schroth, p168
"The class of 1940…into bed."	Wikipedia.com Oral History, Peter A. Carlesimo
"Monday, October 28… none of that."	Gannon, p232

"Father Gannon....your Centenary."	*The Ram*, October 31, 1940
"The centenary celebration...fall day."	Gannon, p142-143, 230-232 Schroth, p184-185
"It all seemed...sources of help."	Gannon, p229

Chapter VIII

Passage	**Source**
"On December 7, 1941...the war."	Fordham.edu
"Gannon was...of General Studies."	Gannon, p239-240
"In 1943...in 1934."	Schroth, p178
"When, in 1907...half of them."	*Woodstock Letters*, 1904, 1907
"The business at hand...thereafter."	Gannon, p241 Oral History, Dr. Andrew B. Myers
"More than...by Clauss."	Schroth, p190
"The priest...theatre productions."	Gannon, 247-248 Interview with Jack Phelan, class of 1954, and former chairman of the Fordham University Communications Department
"Today the station...broadcasting."	Fordham.edu
"That fact...off to college."	Interview with Frank Corbin, class of 1950 and former adjunct communications instructor, Fordham University
"Rev. William Reilly...group to teach."	Oral History, Rev. William Reilly, S.J.
"Denis McInerney...congenial group."	Oral History, Denis McInerney

Passage	Source
"The post…G-Man outfit."	Corbin interview
	Wikipedia.org
"Another well-known…back home."	Interview with Maria Riva and Peter Riva
	Corbin interview
"In 1946…its blessing."	Gannon, p251-252
	Fordham.edu
"Truman's visit…each year."	Fordham.edu
Truman text	Courtesy of the Harry S. Truman Library & Museum, Independence, MO
"As his long…didn't help."	*The New York Times*, *"Big-time by Gannon; Fordham President Declares University Does Not Want a Top Eleven Again; School Got No Benefits; He Tells of Alumni Protests and Scores Sports Writers as 'Tyrants of Tyrants,'"* October 20, 1947
"One of…Jean Lalande."	Gannon, p261
	Fordham.edu

Chapter IX

Passage	Source
"McGinley ended…financial losses."	Gannon, p256-257
	Wikipedia.org
	The Harvard Crimson, *"Fordham Drops Football,"* December 16, 1954
	The Ram, *"1500 Honor Hyatt,"* October 9, 1952,
"A more specific…our heart."	David Maraniss. *When Pride Still Mattered*, New York, Simon & Schuster, 2010
"In these days…true today."	Oral History, Rev. J. Quentin Lauer, S.J.
"Classes…frowned upon."	Oral History, Norman O. Smith

"It wasn't…totalitarian ideologies."   Oral History, William Reilly

"Though the…senior year."   Wikipedia.org
    Gannon, p270

"Rev. Joseph…$1.25."   Oral History, Joseph Frese

"For teachers…school year."

"One student…their own?"   Alan Alda. *Things I Overheard While Talking to Myself*: New York, Random House, 2007

""Best-selling…ascetic."   *The New York Times, "A Talk with Don DeLillo,"* October 10, 1982

"Father Schroth…were gone."   Schroth, p229

"During…in Korea."   Gannon, p266, 272

"Several students…assistant coach."   *The Ram, "Government, Positively,"* September 28, 1950, p4

"As the U.S…not flourishing."   Oral History, Rev. Walter Jaskievicz, S.J.

"A 1952 graduate…1980's."   Schroth, p215-216
    G. Gordon Liddy. *Will*: New York, St. Martin's Press, 1991

"As the…Alumni Association."   Fordham.edu

"Among…always live."   The American Presidency Project, *"Remarks of the Vice President at Fordham University,"* Bronx Gym, Bronx, New York, October 5, 1960, www.presidency.ucsb.edu

"In the late…flee."   Robert Caro. *The Power Broker*: New York, Knopf, 1974

"Father McGinley…of acres."   Oral History Project, Rev. Laurence J. McGinley, S.J.

"Officially…other entities."   Schroth, p242-244

Chapter X

Passage	Source
"In May 1960…1969."	Schroth, p241
"Attorney General…understand it."	www.justice.gov/ag/rfkspeeches/1961/11-18-1961.pdf
"Simultaneous…McGinley Center."	Fordham.edu
"The year 1962…at all."	Gannon, p278
"After a long…football program."	Schroth, p255-256
"Jim Lansing…age of 81."	*The New York Times, "Jim Lansing, 81, Fordham Athlete and Coach,"* December 9, 2000
"Father O'Keefe…Southern Blvd."	Fordham.edu
"Harry Stanton…St. John's University."	Interview with Harry Stanton, class of 1966
"First, there were…fill classrooms."	Schroth, p277
"There was…insurance policy."	Harry Stanton interview
"Father John Donohue…of himself."	Oral History, Rev. John Donohue, S.J.
"Father O'Keefe…the men."	Oral History, Rev. Vincent O'Keefe, S.J.
	Harry Stanton Interview
"The name…Christian gentlemen."	Oral History, Rev. John Donohue, S.J.
"In the tradition…interviewed."	Harry Stanton interview
"Gerri Cunningham…football games."	Interview with Gerri Cunningham Paré, Thomas More College, class of 1968
"According to…like it."	Oral History, George Seuffert
"Paré, through…I was."	Gerri Cunningham Paré interview

239

"It was during…same thing."	Oral History, Rev. Vincent O'Keefe, S.J.
"Not long…World War II."	Harry Stanton interview Fordham.edu
"By late 1965…125 years old."	Fordham.edu
"Frank Corbin…evolution."	Frank Corbin interview
"Father McLaughlin…his students."	Oral History, Stella Moundas
"In response…1974."	Schroth
"Dr. Philip Freund…Marshall McLuhan."	Oral History, Philip Freund, Ph.D.
"McLuhan was…mid 70's."	John Phelan Interview
"Norma Vavolizza…Class of 1968."	Interview with Norma Vavolizza, Thomas More College, class of 1969
"Gerri Paré…five years earlier."	Gerri Cunningham Paré interview
"A year later…arms race."	Fordham University Archives
"President Nixon… on campus."	Wikipedia.org Schroth, p281, 284-285,
"The university's…peace existed."	Wikipedia.org
"Just before…on campus."	*Associated Press*, December 5, 1968
"Still another…said Wilkes."	Fordham Press Release: *"Fordham Remembers Marty Meade, Resilient Dean During Trying Times,"* May 8, 2013
"There was even…if it chose."	Oral History, Andrew B. Myers, Ph.D.
"In March…Selma, Alabama."	Schroth, p281

| "Father McLaughlin...December 1968." | Schroth, p287-289 |
| "Dr. McLaughlin...something dangerous." | *The New York Times*, *"Leo McLaughlin, Jesuit Teacher, Dies at 84,"* August 18, 1996 |

Chapter XI

Passage	**Source**
"The reorganized board...a chapel."	*The New York Times*, *"Laymen to control Fordham Trustees,"* October 31, 1968 Various interviews Walter Gelhorn, *The Sectarian College and the Public Purse:* Oceana Publications, 1970
"Father Walsh...$2 million."	Oral History, Felix Larkin
"In October 1969...our society."	Oral History, Rev. Michael Walsh, S.J.
"The New York...higher education."	Oral History, Paul Reiss
"That demonstration...their classes."	*The Ram*, *"Protest is Debated as Students Await Arrest,"* and *"Students for Campus Peace Demonstrate to Show Support for University Actions,"* November 18, 1969, p1
"According to...gave way."	Oral History, Philip Freund, Ph.D. Christopher Hewitt, *Political Violence and Terrorism in Modern America: A Chronology,* Praeger, 2005
"Felix Larkin...in the hospital."	Oral History, Felix Larkin
"Like thousands...into the world."	Interview with Paul Phelan, Class of 1982

"The 30th president...holiday spirit."	Oral History, Stella Moundas
	Oral History, Rev. James C. Finlay, S.J.
"Dr. Reiss...most universities."	Oral History, Paul Reiss
"In addition to...as an undergraduate."	*The New York Times, "Rev. James C. Finlay, 70, Dies,"* December 7, 1992
	Oral History, Rev. James C. Finlay, S.J.
"Richard Sheehan...known about it."	Interview with Richard J. Sheehan, Class of 1988
"Paul Phelan said...differences."	Paul Phelan interview
"Father Robert Roth...with values."	Oral History, John Olin
"Enrollment, particularly...were relaxed."	Schroth, p319
"Father Quentin Lauer...are now."	Oral History, Rev. J. Quentin Lauer, S.J.
"Finlay put $24 million...better for all."	Oral History, Rev. James C. Finlay, S.J.
"Construction took place...finally extended."	Fordham.edu
"Finlay purchased...parking structure."	*The Ram, "University Purchases Hospital Land,"* September 21, 1978, p1
"Athletics suffered...to Fordham."	Wikipedia.org
"This point...late 80's."	*The New York Times, "Manager of WFUV at Fordham, Ralph Jennings, Retires after 26 Years,"* June 28, 2011
"These were...young doctor."	*ESPN Playbook, "Meet Denzel Washington the Hoops Stud,"* March 21, 2013
"The backslide...similar actions."	Oral History, Rev. James C. Finlay, S.J.

Chapter XII

Passage	Source
"Prior to coming...a total outsider."	Fordham.edu
"Rev. Peter O'Brien...ax to grind, either."	*CLC Observer*, *"Trustees Pick Jesuit Editor,"* March 28, 1984, p1
"A number of years...inspirational force."	*The New York Times, "Jesuits Discuss Future "Age of Laity,"* November 1, 1989
"He also charged...these prizes."	Schroth, p343
"O'Hare created...the university."	*The New York Times, "Cardinal Avery Dulles is Dead,"* December 13, 2008
"In his inaugural address...in the country."	Fordham.edu
"Jack Coffey field...at Lincoln Center."	Fordham.edu
"When O'Hare...development."	Fordham.edu, *"Fordham President Rev. Joseph A. O'Hare, SJ, to Retire,"* May 28, 2002

Chapter XIII

Passage	Source
"And so...goals for Fordham."	Fordham.edu
"Only in...around the world."	Wikipedia.org
"The Greek-lettered...New York."	Wikipedia.org
"Central to McShane's...by injustice."	Fordham.edu
"To that end...community outreach."	Fordham.edu
"As the university...Harrison campus."	Strategic Plan Review Committee. *Progress Report on Integrated Strategic Plan "Toward 2016,"* Rep. Fordham

	University, 2010
	http://chronicle.com/article/Fordham-U-Sells-Marymount/40481
	Fordham.edu
"Fordham maintains… room and board."	Fordham.edu
	U.S. News & World Report (http://colleges.usnews.rankingsandreviews.com/best-colleges/fordham-university-2722)
	Bloomberg Businessweek (http://www.businessweek.com/interactive_reports/ugtable_3-20.html)
"Fordham is…Harvard and Princeton."	*Catholic Education Daily, "Jesuit Colleges Among Most Expensive,"* August 20, 2013
"Almost a century…in the U.S."	*MSNBC* (http://www.msnbc.msn.com/id/26658838/ns/travel-destination_travel/t/pretty-college-campuses/)
"Will Zawacki…of cancer."	Interview with Will Zawacki, class of 2013

Index

247

248

251

255